The Russian Orthodox Church Abroad & The Genuine Orthodox Christians of Greece: A History

First Edition 2023
ISBN: 979-886-045-9076

www.orthodoxtraditionalist.com

Chief Editor: Maria Spanos, B.A.
Cover Design: George Weis
Archivist & Historian: Christophoros Gorman

Dedication

This volume is dedicated to my friends in the Russian Orthodox Church Abroad and the Genuine Orthodox Christians of Greece, who provided me with their in-depth knowledge on this subject and access to their invaluable historical archives which made this book possible.

Table of Contents

Metropolitan Anthony (Khrapovitsky) First-Hierarch of the Russian Orthodox Church Outside of Russia - (1863-1936)

His Eminence Metropolitan Demetrius of America

Introduction

If we carefully examine the history of the Church, we will find that heresies arise in every generation; and during the tumultuous times of heresy, the Lord raises up men who defend the faith. There are two things in particular which characterize these men of God. The first thing is unity (or purity) of the faith, and the second is the unity of the faithful. It cannot be one or the other, but both. Some — apparently those who fight heresy in the wrong spirit — ironically, become heretics themselves, while others become schismatics. But many who, in the right spirit and in good faith, wish to preserve themselves from the venom of heresy, flee the heretics. Many foresee the direction before things become abundantly clear, and the Lord in His mercy, shows signs and miracles to direct the faithful along the path of salvation. We find this in the appearance of the Cross in 1925, one year after the change of the calendar and other signs and miracles followed.

Although the history of the Genuine Orthodox Christians (GOC) seems a little shaky at times, one needs to remember that the entire history of the Church has been shaky at times. Especially in its pursuit to defend the faith; it's par for the course. There is always a period of confusion when heresy enters into the Church. One needs also to realize that we have an enemy, who wishes to destroy the Church; he goes where he feels threatened. But the Lord always prevails, and His Church will prevail, as She has many times, "For there must be also heresies among you, that they which are approved may be made manifest among you." (1 Corinthians, 11:19)

For this reason, I appreciate and recommend this present book. I consider it a very balanced and honest witness of the events from someone who is not officially an "Old Calendarist." Subdeacon Nektarios has the right attitude. He knows that we, the GOC, are truly Orthodox. He is concerned for the unity of the faith, and he wants to get this timely message out, for the days are evil. He is able to discern through the confusion by using the compass of the holy men of ROCOR. He is a voice of reason to those who are in ROCOR-MP, reminding them that we were once in Communion.

May the Lord preserve Subdeacon Nektarios in humility, protect him from the malice of the evil one, and reward him for his labors. The GOC has many Saints who were marvelous men of prayer, truth, and witness. Many of them were clairvoyant, some had the gift of foreknowledge, some were Fools for Christ's Sake, Confessors of Orthodoxy, and Martyrs for the faith. And they are not schismatic saints, for there can be no schismatic saints! Subdeacon Nektarios clearly points out the important fact that the ROCOR clearly accepted the GOC, and so they also accepted her Saints. In fact, Vladyka Averky, of blessed memory, referred to us as "the closest in spirit" to the Russian Church Abroad.

However, that is for another article. For our purposes here, most know concerning Saint Hieronymos of Aegina. He was a man who had an exceptional gift of clairvoyance and foreknowledge, and who left the new calendar church after a Revelation from God! This is a well-known fact which should never be manipulated. So, can you imagine: what would Saint Hieronymos have done if he lived in America and saw what is going on here?

We should pray that love for the Church of Christ may shine in our hearts and uproot the passions which affect our understanding. The facts should not be filtered by our passions, but our passions should be filtered by, and in, the Love of Christ, and His Holy Church. This will help us all to perceive things better. People like Father Seraphim (Rose), of blessed memory, who recognized the Old Calendarists, thought in this way. He lived through some of their most tumultuous times, but was very interested in their state of affairs since he considered them brothers in Christ. Although he foresaw that the one faction (and those influenced by them) would eventually become schismatics, he said concerning the two factions: "This whole quarrel among the Greek Old Calendarists is very unfortunate. Besides involving personalities, which only clouds things, the real issues involved are very subtle and delicate ones that require much tact and patience and love, not theological and canonical tirades" (Letter March 2/15, 1974). He also said: "The two sides quote canons back and forth, when what is needed is love and understanding — and that statement, I realize, could have come straight from the lips of some ecumenist, which only shows how difficult the true path of Orthodoxy has become in our days" (Letter April 24/May 7, 1974).

To those who claim that the GOC are graceless schismatics who are separated from the Church: you should carefully reexamine your stance. Take into consideration the Saints who were either supporters of, or members of the GOC. One is not called a schismatic if he separates for matters of faith. We are not talking about a small heresy here or there, but what our contemporary Saints call, "the heresy of heresies," Ecumenism! There has never been such a heresy in the past; the conditions are unique.

I pray that this book is a witness to all of those who do not belong to the GOC. I pray that God illuminates the minds of all those who have not understood the good intentions and the Orthodoxy of Faith of the men and women who were and are members of the Church of Christ. Lastly, I pray that you all understand the significance of the role of the GOC. Her preservation of the truth is crucial in these evil days.

The Apostle Paul tells us: "Wherefore he saith, awake thou that sleepest, and arise from the dead, and Christ shall give thee light. See then that ye walk circumspectly, not as fools, but as wise, Redeeming the time, because the days are evil. Wherefore be ye not unwise, but understanding what the will of the Lord is." (Ephesians 5:14-17)

May our Lord Jesus Christ unite all Orthodox Christians into the one flock of Jesus Christ. Amen.

With blessings,

† *Metropolitan Demetrius of America*

Church of the Genuine Orthodox Christians of America

Preface

H istory for many people is something they do not invest very much time into learning. For the majority of people history has all but been relegated to the backburner of their interests as something that does not affect the present and does not personally affect them, therefore it is of non-importance. Most people do not study history outside of what was compulsory in grade school or high school, let alone volunteering for any type of formal education in history at the collegiate undergraduate or graduate level. How many of us have seen on social media videos of people quizzing others on elementary historical questions about the United States asking them such things as how many states are there, what year was the United States founded, or even what the Capital of the United States is and with sad results — most cannot even answer those simple questions. Unfortunately, this same lack of historical interest has greatly seeped into the culture of the Orthodox Church among the laity and to a lesser degree the clergy.

Today most people's attention spans are greatly diminished. According to a study by the American Psychological Association, the attention span of someone using a screen device in 2004 was 2.5 minutes on average. In 2012 that decreased to 75 seconds, and within the last five years that had fallen even further to around 47 seconds on average.[1] These unfortunate statistics show that people have a real struggle in devoting the proper time and attention to learning with due diligence the historical realities of many different subjects, including Church History which is an even more niche area of study that is very difficult to investigate because of its small nature.

[1]   Dr. Gloria Mark. "Speaking of Psychology: Why our attention spans are shrinking, with Gloria Mark, PhD," American Psychological Association, accessed June 16th, 2023, https://www.apa.org/news/podcasts/speaking-of-psychology/attention-spans

These statistics have a great effect on us in the Orthodox Church largely because Orthodox Christians cannot afford to not know and understand history. Promulgating the evangelism efforts of the Orthodox Church requires us to know history to a certain degree; there is no way around this. Merely learning history from social media posts, memes, telegram discussions, tweets, or TikTok and YouTube reels is not sufficient in this effort. Which brings us to the problem at discussion.

Unbeknownst to many people, they have recently been presented with the very unknown, but very well documented history of the Genuine Orthodox Christians of Greece and their long history and relationship with the Russian Orthodox Church Outside of Russia (ROCOR). This very small and unknown subject of Orthodox Church history spanning from the 1930s to 2006 is primarily discussed among those historical and academically minded so-called Old Calendarist Orthodox Christians, in smaller circles within the Russian Orthodox Church Outside of Russia (such as myself), and certainly never in any of the New Calendarist jurisdictions. When presented with this history the most universal default reaction by most Orthodox Christians, particularly those in the modernist New Calendarist jurisdictions who know little to nothing about the history of ROCOR and its relationship with the Old Calendar Church, is an aggressive attack against these Orthodox Christians and even against those in the Russian Church Abroad who maintain the position of our Church Fathers such as Saint John (Maximovitch) of San Francisco, blessed Metropolitan Philaret (Voznesensky) of New York, and Archbishop Averky (Taushev) and others.

I present to you this subject as a historian and as historically objective as I can so that you are able to, in the words of Metropolitan Demetrius of the Genuine Orthodox Christians of America, "think objectively, to have a little bit of critical thinking, perhaps open-mindedness," for a better historical understanding of a very complex subject and to cease promulgating un-Orthodox behavior and attitudes to those who share our Orthodox Christian faith and also desire the defeat of the heresy of ecumenism among the Orthodox Church everywhere.[2] This history is by no means exhaustive but will be my small offering to help people think more critically, historically, and compassionately about our true brothers and sisters in Christ.

2   Metropolitan Demetrius of America, "Questions About the GOC to Metropolitan Demetrius - The Light of ROCOR," Orthodox Tradition - YouTube Channel, accessed June 16th, 2023. https://www.youtube.com/watch?v=JaQeq4VVtzM

*The Appearance of the Sign of the Cross over the Church of Saint John
the Theologian, Athens, Greece, 1925*

Chapter I

The Greek Old Calendarist Church & The Seeds of Dialogue with ROCOR

The history of the relationship between the Russian Church Abroad and the Greek Old Calendarist Churches is a long history which stretches from 1926 until roughly 2007 when the Russian Orthodox Church Abroad came into communion with what a few of the ROCOR First-Hierarchs believed[3] to be a Soviet-created Moscow Patriarchate.[4] The beginnings of the Old Calendar Resistance Movement began to take shape in Greece April of 1926 and the relationship and dialogue with the Russian Orthodox Church Abroad shortly thereafter. The history of this dialogue begins with the entrance of the Ecumenical Patriarchate into the modern 20th century ecumenical movement, first with a heretical encyclical and then with the calendar innovation. The genesis of this story begins with "the Church of Constantinople under Patriarchal *locum tenens*, Metropolitan Dorotheos of Prusa, and ten other Metropolitans (Archbishops) [who] published an Encyclical entitled 'To the Churches of Christ Wheresoever They Might Be,' addressing the [heretical] denominations outside the Holy Orthodox Church as 'fellow heirs and partakers of the same promise of God in Jesus Christ.' The title of this Encyclical already presupposed that the Church was not one; its intent was to open an ecumenical dialogue with all the different heterodox bodies on an equal footing. The first item in this agenda proposed the adoption of a common festal calendar so that all the 'Churches' could

---

3   Philaret of New York, "About the New Martyrs and the Gracelessness of the Soviet False Church," circa 1964-1985, *Russian Orthodox Church Outside of Russia*, Audio Recording, 23:29, From the Private Library of Subdeacon Nektarios Harrison, M.A.

4   Central Intelligence Agency (CIA), "Religion," in American Society of Civil Engineers & R.I. Society of Professional Engineers Inc, accessed August 7th, 2023, https://www.cia.gov/readin-groom/docs/NEW%20ENGLAND%20THE%20CRADLE%20OF%5B15877520%5D.pdf

celebrate the great Christian feasts simultaneously"[5] whereby taking the first steps into the heresy of modern ecumenism.

In 1924 when the New Calendar innovation was forced upon the Greek Orthodox Christians in Greece by the infamous heresiarch Meletios Metaxakis it was with the cooperation of the Government and the State Church of Greece. At that time, almost all of the clergy of the Church of Greece submitted to this non-canonical innovation. It was only the Holy Fathers on Mount Athos and those very pious lay people and some clergy (readers, subdeacons, deacons, and priests) who refused to bend their knee to this sudden change in the traditional Church calendar. From 1924-1935 it was these pious Orthodox Christians alone who resisted without the protective omophorion of an Orthodox hierarch. These Orthodox Christians who refused to accept the non-canonical calendar innovation began to be persecuted by the State Church of Greece for refusing to accept the New Calendar, one example being the martyrdom of Catherine Routis, who was struck in the head by the Greek Police for attending an Old Calendarist vespers service.

"On April 24, 1926, the State Church of Greece issued a very hard encyclical (Protocol Number 2398/2203) directed against the traditional Orthodox Christians. The encyclical states: They separate themselves from the Church and cut themselves off from the Body of Christ, drawing upon themselves condemnation and excommunication, not knowing, or perhaps forgetting, that he who does not hear the Church is 'as the heathen man and the publican' (Matt. 18:17)... The decisions of the Church are absolutely obligatory; he who does not obey them no longer belongs to her, he is deprived of the means of divine grace; he is separated and cut off from her, and is liable to eternal torment."[6]

5   The Holy Orthodox Church in North America, *The Struggle Against Ecumenism: The History of the True Orthodox Church of Greece from 1924-1994* (Boston: Holy Transfiguration Monastery, 1998), 23.
6   Ibid., 39-41.

Despite this targeted encyclical against the community of Orthodox Christians in Greece who were actively resisting the calendar innovation, they continued on in their struggle without a bishop until 1935. On May 25th, 1935, the community of Old Calendar Orthodox Christians requested of three different Greek Orthodox Bishops to take their community under their omophorion. These three bishops were Metropolitan Germanus of Demetrias, the retired Metropolitan Chrysostom of Florina, and Metropolitan Chrysostom of Zakynthos. These three bishops who had actively been trying to return the Church of Greece to the traditional Church calendar, to no avail, agreed to take the community under their protection and formed the Old Calendar Church of Greece which elected Metropolitan Germanus as their synodal first-hierarch.[7] This in brief is how the Genuine Orthodox Church of Greece and the Old Calendarist movement began.

Now at this early stage (1920-1935) the ROCOR involvement was itself very limited. This was because, as I previously mentioned, the heretical encyclical issued by synod of the Ecumenical Patriarchate, 'To the Churches of Christ Wheresoever They Might Be,' was published in 1920, the non-canonical calendar change took place in 1924, and the official formation of the Old Calendar Church of Greece under the omophorion of Orthodox Hierarchs did not take place until May of 1935.

---

7   "New Zion in Babylon: The Orthodox Church in the Twentieth Century (Part III)," Dr. Vladimir Moss, PhD, accessed June 27th, 2023, https://www.academia.edu/10287412/NEW_ ZION_IN_BABYLON_PART_3_1925_1941_

It should be noted however, that this encyclical at the time did not have far-reaching effects outside of the Greek world and according to Metropolitan Germanus of Demetrias he had requested this publication "three times for the documents of the Patriarchates to be deposited and they were not deposited, therefore they were not read, so that I and the Hierarchy could be enlightened. The 1920 Encyclical, although printed, was not disseminated and it was only in 1949 that it gradually became known."[8]

With the Russian Orthodox Church Outside of Russia itself only having been formed in 1920, the interaction with those in the Old Calendar resistance movement at these early stages was very limited. However, the first interactions we do have are archived letters from Metropolitan Anthony (Khrapovitsky), the very first First-Hierarch of the Russian Church Abroad, who wrote multiple letters to a monk on Mount Athos concerning the Old Calendar movement in 1926, nine years before the actual formation of the Genuine Orthodox Church of Greece. In this letter below it can be seen that Metropolitan Anthony was not in favor of the resistors ceasing commemoration of the New Calendar bishops at the time of his writing. It can be surmised from the language in the letters that because this innovation that divided the Church of Greece (contemporaneously with his writing) was in fact still a fresh issue, that he might have expected that a council would rectify the situation sooner rather than later, let alone over one-hundred years later and counting. Nevertheless, Metropolitan Anthony in Letter No. 98 to Hieroschemamonk Theodosius of Mount Athos, writes:

And Christ is and will be among us.

Honorable Father Theodosius,

I have never approved of the new style nor those who adhere to

---

[8] Nikolaos Mannis, *The Ecclesiology of the Metropolitan Chrysostomos: Presentation of the Ecclesiological Positions of the Former Florentine Confessor, Chrysostomos (Kavouridou) (†1955) in the Form of Questioning* (Athens: Genuine Orthodox Christians of Greece, 2012), 7-8.

this style. I hope that if we overcome our ecclesiastical turbulence, the Church, under the threat of excommunication, will demand a return to the old style. However, you are surely aware of the 13th canon of the First-Second Council, which imposed the deprivation of the priesthood on clergy who break communion with their Metropolitan before being judged. That is why I was disappointed that your followers do not receive antidoron in the new-style monasteries. You, especially, should have been cautious, as neither you nor those with you have bishops who share your views, thus approaching the priestless and, at the very least, schismatics in general.

Your zeal is praiseworthy, but self-will and anticipating judgment on the hierarchs are hardly praiseworthy. Finally, the canons prohibit joint prayer with heretics and schismatics, and by continuing the latter but not accepting antidoron as a sign of communion, you introduce something new and enticing.

While sincerely respecting your fasting endeavors, I would like an explanation for these actions, if you do not consider it beneath you, as well as forgiveness from you for my direct words.

I request your holy prayers, invoking God's blessing upon you, and seeking forgiveness on the Holy Forty, I remain your sincere well-wisher.[9]

Metropolitan Anthony.

March 8/21, 1932.

"The cunning one, having sown the seeds of heretical weeds in the Church of Christ, and seeing that they are cut off by the sword of the Spirit from the root, he, having entered upon another path of deception, attempts with the madness of schismatics to sever the body of Christ. But the holy Council, having completely condemned this intention of his, has now decided: If any presbyter or deacon, based on certain

---

[9] "Letter No. 98. To Hieroschemamonk Theodosius of Mount Athos," Азбукаверы, accessed June 28th, 2023. https://azbyka.ru/otechnik/Antonij_Hrapovickij/pisma/#0_100

accusations, dares to separate himself from communion with his Bishop before the investigation and examination by the Council, and before his condemnation is completed, and he does not raise his name in the sacred prayers during the liturgies, according to the ecclesiastical tradition, let such a person be subjected to excommunication and be deprived of all priestly honors. For the presbyter ordained and assuming the authority of the judge, entrusted to the Metropolitan, and by himself condemning his father and Bishop before the judgment, is unworthy of both the honor and the name of a presbyter. And those who follow such a person, if they are certain of the clergy, shall likewise be deprived of their honor. But if they are monks or laypeople, let them be completely excommunicated from the Church until they renounce communion with the schismatics and return to their Bishop."[10]

Metropolitan Anthony writing in Letter No. 99 to Hieroschemamonk Theodosius, writes:

Truly, Christ has risen!

Rejoice! It is heard from everywhere that the Greeks want to return to the old style, and then your perplexity will end. Of course, I completely disagree with your arguments. The question remains about what to recognize as a sacred tradition, and by acknowledging its violations, let's say among the Greeks, we should pose another question: does such a violation deserve a church schism or only admonishment? Father, you are one step away from falling into delusion; may the Mother of God protect you from further steps. I am writing to you as a friendly friend, so that you do not ruin your 40-year struggle with schism in the Church on the basis of external conditional formalism, and moreover, an arbitrary one. The New Style is no less repugnant to me than it is to you, but even more repugnant is the defection from Orthodoxy and its hierarchy by self-loving monks. However, God will grant that this

---

10   "Letter No. 98. To Hieroschemamonk Theodosius of Mount Athos," Азбука веры, accessed June 28th, 2023, https://azbyka.ru/otechnik/Antonij_Hrapovickij/pisma/#0_100

will end soon with the victorious triumph of the old style over the new. I am certainly not invited to the council.[11] The Greeks have grown to hate me for not sympathizing with their insolence, and they don't even mention my name in correspondence regarding the upcoming council matters. Besides expressing my disapproval of the new style, I have not mentioned anything and do not wish to get involved in this matter. I ask for your holy prayers and remain your well-wisher.

Metropolitan Anthony.

Christ has risen! I greet you with the celebration of the radiant Christ's Resurrection.

April 18, 1932.[12]

The context of Metropolitan Anthony's letter to Hieroschemamonk Theodosius is that he is writing concerning ceasing commemoration of the New Calendar Bishops in Greece and the Patriarch of Constantinople. As with the rest of the Old Calendar priests who joined the resistance movement, they ceased commemoration of the Patriarch and other New Calendar Bishops because of the perceived schism that was created by Meletios Metaxakis' innovation. Metropolitan Anthony, in agreeing that the new calendar was repugnant, to use his words, was not at this period in time in agreement with ceasing communion with the New Calendarists or the Patriarch. As we can see from the previous history examined, the heretical encyclical 'To the Churches of Christ Wheresoever They Might Be' that was signed and published by the Synod of the Patriarchate of Constantinople was little-known to most of the Greek Orthodox hierarchs, so in all probability it would not have been known to Metropolitan Anthony as well; which would have deprived him of additional historical context concerning the problematic road the Ecumenical Patriarchate was beginning to travel down. What is not in the context of this letter is the

---

11 This refers to the then planned future Ecumenical Council that never came to fruition

12 "Letter No. 99. To Hieroschemamonk Theodosius," Азбука веры, accessed June 28th, 2023, https://azbyka.ru/otechnik/Antonij_Hrapovickij/pisma/#0_101

subject of parallel jurisdictions which is defaulted to by many Orthodox Christians in the modernist jurisdictions. These letters by Metropolitan Anthony were penned March-April of 1932 at which point in time the Old Calendar Synod was not yet in existence and so, for these letters, this topic was not yet on the table for discussion.

On October 11th, 1934, George Paraschos and Basil Stamatoulis, the President and Secretary General of the Community of Genuine Orthodox Christians, in the attempt to officially come under the omophorion of an Orthodox Hierarch, appealed to the ROCOR Synod and Metropolitan Anthony with the hopes that he would consecrate bishops for them. However, nothing came of this, presumably because by this time Metropolitan Anthony's health was in decline.[13]

Metropolitan Anthony would repose in the Lord, in August 1936, twenty-one months after this petition from the Old Calendarists in Greece and just fifteen months after the establishment of the Synod of the Genuine Orthodox Church of Greece.

After the repose of Metropolitan Anthony, the Russian Orthodox Church Abroad elected as the First-Hierarch Anastasius (Gribanovsky) in 1936. Metropolitan Anastasius, when it came to the ROCOR policy concerning the Church calendar, remained closely in line with his predecessor Metropolitan Anthony. Metropolitan Anastasius says concerning the new calendar innovation that, "Our Church remains loyal to the use of the old calendar and considers the introduction of the new calendar to be an error. Nonetheless, its tactic was always to preserve spiritual unity with Orthodox Churches, even those who have adopted the new calendar, but only to the degree to which they celebrate Pascha in compliance with the decision of the First Ecumenical Council. Our Church has never labeled the Ecumenical Patriarchate or the Greek

---

13   "New Zion in Babylon: The Orthodox Church in the Twentieth Century (Part III)," Dr. Vladimir Moss, PhD, accessed June 27th, 2023, https://www.academia.edu/10287412/NEW_ZION_IN_BABYLON_PART_3_1925_1941_

Archdiocese of North and South America as schismatic, and never abrogated spiritual union with them."[14]

However, this would unfortunately change within the Russian Church Abroad because of the heretical ecumenism that these modernist jurisdictions would further go into such that "her ties with her sister Old Calendar Churches in Greece, Rumania and Bulgaria [would be] supported and strengthened."[15]

---

14   "The Development of Russian Orthodox Church Outside of Russia's Attitude Toward Other Local Orthodox Churches and Non-Orthodox Christians," ROCOR Studies: Historical Studies of the Russian Church Abroad, accessed June 28th, 2023, https://www.rocorstudies.org/2008/11/18/the-development-of-russian-orthodox-church-outside-of-russias-attitude-to-ward-other-local-orthodox-churches-and-non-orthodox-christians/
15   Michael Rodzianko, Rassaphor-Monk Vsevolod, *The Truth About the Russian Church Abroad* (Jordanville: Printshop of St. Job of Pochaev - Holy Trinity Monastery, 2002), 51.

Chapter II

The Russian Orthodox Church Abroad & The Old Calendar Hierarchal Revival

Over the course of time and no doubt through God's providence, Father Petros (Astyfides), a key figure of the Greek Old Calendar movement in the United States, while traveling through Grand Central Station, on December 25th, 1954, would come across Archbishop Averky of Jordanville and Archbishop Leonty of Chile, both of whom were on their way to Holy Trinity Monastery. As circumstance happens, these three traditional Orthodox clergymen were taking the same train north through Manhattan. It was on this day in 1954 that sparked a life-long friendship between Archbishop Averky, Archbishop Leonty, and Father Petros who would later be consecrated to the episcopacy by Archbishop Leonty in the Cathedral of Saint Markella in Astoria, New York.

After the traditionalist Greek Orthodox Christians learned of the Russian Orthodox Church Outside of Russia, whom they also saw as resistors to the calendar change, modernism, and the heresy of ecumenism, they eventually petitioned Metropolitan Anastasius (Gribanovsky) and the Holy Synod to consecrate for them bishops for their Church. However, Metropolitan Anastasius, not wanting to get involved in Greek jurisdictional affairs, always turned them down. This, however, did not spoil the friendship between the Russian and Greek clergymen that was created that fateful day on the feast of St. Spyridon in Grand Central Station.

Now around 1955, the eleven Old Calendarist Orthodox Priests who were living in New York City, still trying to rectify their situation and come under the omophorion of a traditionalist Greek Orthodox hierarch, gathered at the old Church of Saint Nicholas in New York, once located at what is today Ground Zero, and decided to nominate a priest worthy of the episcopacy whom they could present to a traditional Russian bishop for ordination and they chose Father Petros (Astyfides). They approached Archbishop Leonty of Chile who was at the time part of the North American Metropolia. Unfortunately, Archbishop Leonty was still not willing to cross this line as it would have serious ramifications throughout the Orthodox world in the United States and in Europe.

In November of 1959 the Synod of the Russian Church Abroad held a meeting and at this synodal meeting was a discussion concerning those Old Calendarists who sought the help of ROCOR in consecrating bishops. A large majority of the bishops of the time were well in support of these Old Calendarist Orthodox Christians. Those in support of them or at least open to exploring to helping them further were Saint John of San Francisco, Archbishop Averky of Syracuse, Archbishop Alexander of Berlin, and Bishops Nikon, Savva, and Anthony of Los Angeles, whereas Bishop Anthony of Geneva, known for his liberal leanings, was reticent and Metropolitan Anastasius, maintaining the position of his predecessor, was not in support of this, and did not want to cause political waves within other jurisdictions.

Of these synodal members, Archbishop Averky of Syracuse was the most supportive of the Old Calendarists. The minutes of the synod have him recorded saying,

Bishop Averky: Old Calendarists often come to Holy Trinity Monastery. In Athens on the [Feast of the] Exaltation [of the Holy Cross], a crowd of Greeks came out of Athens with a procession, during which the Holy Cross appeared in the sky and photographic pictures were taken. The movement deserves a helping hand.

Bishop Averky: Sees a contradiction in the fact that the new style introduced in Greece is recognized as enemies of Orthodoxy by the French and Romanians. Why do we communicate with them while repelling the Greek Old Believers?

Bishop Averky: Finds Bishop Anthony's reasoning quite logical. However, it must be definitively decided whether we allow the new style for liturgical economy. But this is for others, for our own people, we do not allow it. In our mission in the West, we have to be Greeks, and for our own people, we have to be Jews. But we set ourselves the task of proclaiming the truth to the world. They are drawn to this truth. Therefore, we must support the Old Believers.[16]

And during this meeting Saint John of San Francisco can be seen supporting the statement of Archbishop Seraphim of Chicago who is recorded saying,

Archbishop Seraphim of Chicago: Says he has been interested in this movement for a long time. The Old Calendarists have two or three groups, but the strongest is the one that appeals to us. There is a group with bishops, but improperly ordained [referring to the Matthewites]. He, too, thought the Old Calendarists could get help from the Jerusalem Patriarch, but then he found out this was mistaken. Some fear complications with other Greek churches, but it is possible to conduct the matter in a way that does not cause great complications. However, we must put the truth of the Church above our own interests. Archimandrite Nicholas [Pekatoros] of Washington speaks negatively about the Old Calendarists. On [Mount] Athos, it is said that Archimandrite Nicholas, who himself belonged to the Old Calendarists, does not have a completely objective assessment of this movement. Being a partisan, he must be relegated. The movement

---

16   "The ROCOR Debate at the 1959 Council of Bishops on Consecrating Hierarchs for the Greek Old Calendarists - Protocol #15," Russian Orthodox Church Outside of Russia, accessed June 29th, 2023, http://sinod.ruschurchabroad.org/Arh%20Sobor%201959%20Prot10-16.htm

deserves all the attention and help it can get.[17]

Although a large portion of the members on the synod supported the Old Calendarists they were still cautious moving forward because of the sensitive nature of what was in question and because of the position of Metropolitan Anastasius on the issue. However, even though the synod at that time decided not to act according to the request of those Old Calendar Orthodox Christians, that was not the end of the road. Within the ROCOR there were two bishops who were willing to help them. These two ROCOR bishops knowing that there was a great need for a traditional Old Calendarist Greek Hierarch in Greece, decided to consecrate a traditionalist Orthodox bishop for the Old Calendarist flock. These two bishops were Archbishop Seraphim of Chicago and Bishop Theophil of Detroit. However, they required that their help would be under the conditions of absolute discretion. Eventually, an Old Calendar Orthodox priest from Greece was selected to be consecrated and on December 9th, 1960, in Detroit, Michigan, Archbishops Seraphim and Theophil consecrated Akakios (Papas) who would lead the Genuine Orthodox Christians of Greece.

When this became known to Metropolitan Anastasius, as one can imagine he was not happy. However, this was not the only ordination of Greek Old Calendarists to take place by Hierarchs of the ROCOR. In 1961, Archbishop Leonty of Chile flew to Athens and with the newly consecrated Bishop Akakios (Papas) they consecrated six more bishops for the Genuine Orthodox Christians of Greece. When Archbishop Leonty returned from Greece there eventually was a Synodal meeting held on November 26th, 1962 in which the members of the Synod were, in fact, divided amongst each other as to whether it was proper for Archbishop Leonty to have consecrated bishops for the Greek Old Calendarists and

---

17   "The ROCOR Debate at the 1959 Council of Bishops on Consecrating Hierarchs for the Greek Old Calendarists - Protocol #15," Russian Orthodox Church Outside of Russia, accessed June 29th, 2023, http://sinod.ruschurchabroad.org/Arh%20Sobor%201959%20Prot10-16.htm

in this meeting tempers raged. For example, Archbishop Athanasius of Buenos Aires is recorded in the minutes as "horrified by what has happened. What Archbishop Seraphim says is totally unacceptable. It is not clear to us who Akakios is and on what basis Archbishop Leonty considers him to be a bishop and not an archimandrite. From the canonical point of view, all of this is a gamble, as we have called the consecration of [Basil] Tomaschik. The new Greek Church has now been given a non-canonical start. The matter must be removed from the agenda, placing all responsibility on Archbishop Leonty."[18]

However, Bishop Nikon (Rklitsky) is reported saying, "that on the day of his consecration, he was approached by Greeks to help them leave the Soviet jurisdiction. He is aware of the secret ordinations in the Catacomb Church, and his heart trembles with joy at the news of the Greek Old Calendarists being consecrated. The only thing that caused confusion was the uncertainty as to who had performed the consecration of Bishop Akakios."[19] And in defense of himself, Archbishop Leonty is recorded stating that in the Church Abroad there have been a number of canonical violations. One should fear God more than men. He answers to God for his deed and does not repent.[20]

Now on November 29th, 1962, Archbishop Leonty and Bishop Seraphim of Caracas who had plans to consecrate Archimandrite Petros (Astyfides) in Caracas, Venezuela, at the last minute decided that the consecration would go forth at the Church of Saint Markella's in Astoria, New York, just 5 miles from the ROCOR Synodal headquarters on 93rd Street. When Metropolitan Anastasius and the rest of the Synod of the Russian Church Abroad learned of this consecration they publicly declared that the consecrations by the ROCOR Hierarchs in Greece

---

18   "A Contentious Discussion on the Consecration of Greek Old Calendar Bishops by Archbishop Leonty during the 1962 meeting of the ROCOR Council of Bishops. The Minutes of Protocol #24, November 13/26, 1962," Russian Orthodox Church Outside of Russia, accessed June 29th, 2023, http://sinod.ruschurchabroad.org/Arh%20Sobor%201962%20Prot.htm
19   Ibid.
20   Ibid.

and in Astoria were not recognized. Another Synodal meeting was held on November 30th, 1962, in which the two groups again debated these consecrations done by their fellow hierarchs. This synodal meeting, much like the last one a few days prior, was again heated. Metropolitan Vitaly recalls that "Archbishop Leonty is losing his temper and speaks in an impossibly harsh tone."[21]

Saint John (Maximovitch) during this meeting defends Archbishop Leonty and states, "that the Old Calendarists have been knocking on our door for six years. The Council of Bishops could not take a decision, recognizing this as an internal matter of the Greeks. We must accept Archbishop Leonty's explanations as satisfactory and end the debate there."[22] Archbishop Averky (Taushev) in turn defends Archbishop Leonty saying with great length that:

Standing on the ground of canons, would not himself have dared to perform the consecrations of the Greek Old Calendarists. But at the same time, in his heart he cannot [but] admire the courage with which Archbishop Leonty committed the act for which his conscience called. One cannot help but be against the formal violation of the canons. But in the life of other Churches, we see a continuous violation of the canons. In view of this abnormal general situation, Archbishop Leonty should be treated with leniency. This is further recommended by the fact that there have been a number of illegal acts on the part of the Patriarchate of Constantinople with respect to the Russian Church, such as: the rejection of Poland and the Baltic States, the creation of the Exarchate of Paris, the rejection of Bishops Orestes and Bogdan in America. Now that everything is irrational, there must be a special approach. The canons cannot now be approached legalistically. The canons are for the man, not

---

21   "A Contentious Discussion on the Consecration of Greek Old Calendar Bishops by Archbishop Leonty during the 1962 meeting of the ROCOR Council of Bishops. Minutes of Protocol #28, November 17/30, 1962," Russian Orthodox Church Outside of Russia, accessed June 29th, 2023, http://sinod.ruschurchabroad.org/Arh%20Sobor%201962%20Prot.htm
22   Ibid.

the man for the canons. The Sabbath is for the man, not the man for the Sabbath. One must think of the salvation of souls, not of the observance of the form alone. The form can be Orthodox in appearance and false in substance. In this light, we must evaluate the act of Archbishop Leonty. He performed a courageous act of assistance to a fraternal Church, which is now the closest to us in spirit. The Greek Church is now oppressed and persecuted. It was a great mistake that at one time we were too lenient with the introduction of the new calendar, for it was intended to bring a schism into the Orthodox Church. It was the work of the enemies of the Church of Christ. The fruits are already visible. Even in America, there are Greek clergy who torment their conscience for the adoption of the new calendar. Associated with the observance of the old calendar is the preservation of all kinds of devotions in various areas. Along with the removal of the old calendar is the removal of asceticism from the temple. The Old Calendarists are the ones closest to us in spirit. The only "but" in Archbishop Leonty's action is that he acted, as it were, unbrotherly, in defiance of the decision of the Council, though well-meaning.[23]

As the Synodal meeting of November 30th, 1962, came to a close and the Synod officially drafted a statement which said, "The Russian Church Abroad has never interfered in the affairs of the other autocephalous Churches throughout her existence, and for this reason, in spite of her fraternal sympathy with the Greek Old Calendarists, has continually rejected numerous appeals to her by the Greek Old Calendarists for the consecration of bishops for them. The Council of Bishops greatly regrets the fact that His Grace Leonty, Archbishop of Chile, Santiago, and Peru, in the month of May 1962, contrary to the above, on his own initiative, without the knowledge and permission of the Synod of Bishops and the First-Hierarch, Metropolitan Anastasius, participated in the consecration

---

23   "A Contentious Discussion on the Consecration of Greek Old Calendar Bishops by Archbishop Leonty during the 1962 meeting of the ROCOR Council of Bishops. Minutes of Protocol #28, November 17/30, 1962," Russian Orthodox Church Outside of Russia, accessed June 29th, 2023, http://sinod.ruschurchabroad.org/Arh%20Sobor%201962%20Prot.htm

of Greek Old Calendarists. The Council of Bishops henceforth enjoins the Most Reverend Hierarchs of the Russian Church Abroad to refrain from interfering in the affairs of both the Greek and other Autocephalous Orthodox Churches. As for the participation of some other hierarchs of the Russian Orthodox Church Abroad in the secret consecration of Greek Old Calendarist hierarchs, as indicated in the correspondence on this issue, neither the Synod of Bishops nor the First Hierarch gave any permission to any bishops for such participation, and they are unaware of such consecrations."[24]

Although the Synod officially did not accept these consecrations as a whole, that was not what would be said in private by a large majority of the Hierarchs of the Russian Orthodox Church Outside of Russia. The individual members of the Russian Synod that did recognize these ordinations, albeit in private, were Saint John (Maximovitch), Archbishop Averky of Jordanville, Bishop Nektary of Seattle, Bishop Savvas of Edmonton, Bishop Anthony of Melbourne, and of course Bishops Seraphim of Chicago and Seraphim of Caracas, and Archbishop Leonty of Chile who made the consecrations for the Genuine Orthodox Christians of Greece possible. This private recognition of the consecrations, particularly that of Bishop Petros of Astoria, can be seen by a letter that was written, signed, and is now archived at the Cathedral of Saint Markella in Astoria, New York, which the above bishops wrote to Petros of Astoria, recognizing him as a fellow Orthodox Hierarch saying:

24   "A Contentious Discussion on the Consecration of Greek Old Calendar Bishops by Archbishop Leonty during the 1962 meeting of the ROCOR Council of Bishops. Minutes of Protocol #28, November 17/30, 1962," Russian Orthodox Church Outside of Russia, accessed June 29th, 2023, http://sinod.ruschurchabroad.org/Arh%20Sobor%201962%20Prot.htm

To: His Eminence

Bishop Peter of Astoria

New York City, N.Y.

Your Eminence:

The undersigned are herewith presenting to Your Eminence the expression of their most sincere gratitude for your kind reception and hospitality.

May the Lord have Your Eminence in his protection!

Your living brothers in Christ,

(Signed),

+ John of San Francisco *[In Greek]*

+ Archbishop Leonty

+ Bishop Seraphim

+ Bishop Savva of Edmonton

+ Bishop Nektary

+ Archbishop Averky

+ Bishop Anthony of Melbourne[25]

---

25   "Part 2 of Met. Petros of Astoria - His Life and Struggle," Greek Orthodox Television - YouTube Channel, accessed August 28th, 2023, https://youtu.be/vLt7cY78eaM?si=85uMMUr6zbFG9iXP&t=1997

Chapter III

The Synod of Blessed Metropolitan Philaret of New York & The Recognition of Sister Churches

Now, in 1964 at the Synodal meeting in New York City, Metropolitan Anastasius announced that he would be retiring due to his ailing health and that they needed to choose a new successor to lead the Russian Church Abroad. The Holy Synod elected Bishop Philaret as their new First-Hierarch to succeed the aging Metropolitan Anastasius. "The enthronement of Metropolitan Philaret, which took place on Saturday and Sunday, May 17/30 — 18/31, developed into an unprecedented solemn feast which left a deep and abiding impression upon all. To a degree perhaps never before experienced by such a multitude, participants in this feast felt themselves engulfed by the grace-endowing and holy mystery of the Church. Of great influence was the fact that the entire service, both on Saturday and on Sunday was, so to say, spiritually imbued with the continuing act of elevation to the head of the Church of the new metropolitan."[26] It was shortly thereafter that the ROCOR former First-Hierarch Metropolitan Anastasius reposed in the Lord in May of 1965. Now that Metropolitan Philaret was installed as the First-Hierarch of the Russian Church Abroad, the policy that was maintained by both Metropolitan Anthony and Anastasius would change as Metropolitan Philaret wanted to help unite the Old Calendar Churches as well as come into full eucharistic communion with them.

On November 25th, 1969, the Holy Synod of the Russian Orthodox Church Outside of Russia officially changed its position on the consecrations of the Greek Old Calendarist Bishops that took place in 1960 in Detroit, 1961 in Athens, and in 1962 in Astoria, New York,

---

26   Holy Trinity Monastery, "The Enthronement of Metropolitan Philaret," *Orthodox Life* 87, no. 3 (May-June 1964), 6.

by those few ROCOR Hierarchs. The ROCOR Synod in a document addressed to Archbishop Auxentius and the Holy Synod of the True Orthodox Christians of Greece states that, "The many trials which the Orthodox Church has endured from the beginning of its history are especially great in our evil times, and, consequently, this especially requires unity among those who are truly devoted to the Faith of the Fathers. With these sentiments, we wish to inform you that the Synod of Bishops of the Russian Orthodox Church Abroad recognizes the validity of the episcopal ordinations of your predecessor of blessed memory, the reposed Archbishop Akakios, and the consequent ordinations of your Holy Church. Hence, taking into account also various other circumstances, our hierarchical Synod esteems your hierarchy as brothers in Christ in full communion with us. May the blessing of God rest upon all the clergy and faithful of your Church, especially during the coming days of the Nativity in the flesh of our Lord and Saviour Jesus Christ.[27]

From 1969 forward, the Russian Orthodox Church Abroad under the saintly leadership of Metropolitan Philaret of New York recognized the ordinations of the Genuine Orthodox Christians of Greece that had been performed by those few ROCOR hierarchs several years prior. "ROCOR [now] was in communion with both the Florinite and Matthewite branches of the Greek Old Calendar Church."[28] However, by 1971, Metropolitan Philaret and the Holy Synod of the ROCOR wanted these two groups to unite and to become one Old Calendar Greek Orthodox Church. This desire, however honorable, would eventually break down the already shaky unity that existed because of differences in ecclesiology of the Russian Church Abroad, the Florinite Synod, and the Matthewite Synod. In addition to the differences of opinion concerning

---

27   Holy Synod of the Russian Orthodox Church Outside of Russia, "To The Most Blessed Auxentius, Archbishop of the True Orthodox Christians in Greece," The Orthodox Archive, accessed June 29th, 2023, https://www.theorthodoxarchive.org/post/50th-anniversary-of-the-goc-episcopal-consecrations-by-the-russian-church-abroad

28   Anastasios Hudson, *Metropolitan Petros of Astoria: A Microcosm of the Old Calendar Movement in America* (Reston: Anastasios Hudson, 2014), 44.

ecclesiology as it revolved around the matters of grace in the mysteries in the New Calendar modernist jurisdictions; there was also the matter of the problematic episcopal consecrations of the Matthewite hierarchy by Bishop Matthew who in violation of Canon I of the Apostolic Canons, single-handedly consecrated for himself a synod, despite Canon I explicitly stating, "Let a bishop be ordained by two or three bishops."[29]

These single-handed consecrations were corrected by the Russian Church Abroad on Matthewite Bishops Kallistos and Epiphanios at Holy Transfiguration Monastery in Boston, Massachusetts in September of 1971. According to an official synodal letter penned by Archpriest George (Grabbe) in November of 1973 in which he states, "The Bishops Kallistos and Epiphanios were not ordained by our Synod. They were accepted in communion as bishops with only the laying on of hands on them, already in bishops' vestments, according to the 8 canon of the First Ecumenical Council. That was to rectify beyond doubts the irregularity caused by the founding of their hierarchy through the consecration originally performed by one bishop."[30] This was done with the foregoing agreement that these two bishops would return to Greece and perform the laying on of hands on all of their clergy as to regularize their ordinations as well. However, once they returned to Greece this was immediately rejected by the majority of the Matthewites which ultimately led to their synod breaking communion with the Russian Church Abroad.

Now in 1974 the Florinite Synod, in an attempt to show equal fidelity to the official confession of 1950 and show the Matthewites they were just as strict in their confession, published an encyclical entitled, "Thus Do We Believe, Thus Do We Speak" which denied that the Official State

29   The Canons of the Holy and Altogether August Apostles, "Canon I," in *Nicene & Post-Nicene Fathers, Volume 14*, ed. Philip Schaff & Henry Wace (Peabody: Hendrickson Publications, 1999), 594.
30   "Letter from Archpriest Gregory Grabbe to Mr. V.M. Shallcross, November 7th, 1973," Synod of the Russian Orthodox Church Outside of Russia, accessed June 30th, 2023, https://www.theorthodoxarchive.org/post/bishop-gregory-grabbe-to-mr-shallcross-concerning-metropolitan-kallistos-and-ephiphanios-1973

Church of Greece was without grace in their mysteries. However, Bishop Petros of the Genuine Orthodox Church in America refused to sign this document under the advice of blessed Metropolitan Philaret of New York and the Holy Synod of the Russian Orthodox Church Abroad who had consecrated him to the episcopacy. This refusal to sign this document caused the Synod of the Genuine Orthodox Christians of Greece to remove Metropolitan Petros from the Synod. Metropolitan Petros seeing his Mother Church as the Russian Church applied to them to be received into the Synod of the Russian Church Abroad.

In a letter by Metropolitan Petros of Astoria to the Russian Synod he wrote, "I was ordained by the most holy bishops of the Russian Orthodox Church Outside of Russia, my ordination was recognized by the Russian Synod. From a canonical aspect I should have belonged to the Russian Synod from the time of my ordination, but my heart was set in healing the struggling anti-ecumenist, anti-modernist Old Calendar Church of Greece which is truly suffering greatly from the enemies of the faith. However, I always enjoyed and desired to have communion with my maternal Russian Synod. My communion with the Synod of Greece has been severed and the Russian Holy Synod of Bishops has also severed communion with me ironically enough because I obey and follow its own decrees and I will not sign something the Russian Synod itself condemns.

As for my future canonical position, that I think should be in accordance with the holy canons of the Church in the words of Saint Ignatios the Godbearer, where there is unity there also is Jesus Christ. It is therefore my conviction that the only canonical thing for me and my clergymen to do is ask my brother bishops to accept me into the Holy Council of Bishops of the Russian Orthodox Church Outside of Russia as a full member under the Synod's jurisdiction. Presently, we commemorate Philaret's name during the Proskomedia, but we dearly want to commemorate his name during all services [and] in all Churches.

I consider the Russian Synod an oasis of Orthodoxy in a desert of ecumenism and heresy, and it is for this reason that it is my fondest wish to have ecclesiastical union with you." Tragically, the Russian Synod's refusal left Bishop Petros without membership in any Orthodox Synod of Bishops.[31]

In that same year the Russian Orthodox Church in a Synodal Letter clarified its position on the New Calendar and those modernist jurisdictions using this innovation, saying,

The first resolution of the Holy Council of Bishops of the Russian Orthodox Church Outside of Russia pertaining to the question set forth by the Old-Calendar Church bodies in Greece:

The Russian Orthodox Church Outside of Russia considers the introduction of the new calendar as a mistake, bringing irregularity into the life of the Church and in the final end causing a schism. Therefore, she did not accept it, does not accept it and will not accept it and avoids concelebration with the new calendarists. As to the question regarding the presence of non-existence of grace among the new calendarists, the Russian Orthodox Church Outside of Russia does not regard itself or any local Church as having the authority to reach a final decision, since a definitive ruling in this matter can be made only by a properly convoked, competent Ecumenical Council, with the indispensable participation of a free Church of Russia. 12/25 September 1974.[32]

As the years passed by and the chaos in the Old Calendar Churches began to die down, Bishop Petros was eventually received back into the Synod of the Genuine Orthodox Christians of Greece in 1985. Interestingly, in 1994, the now Metropolitan Petros was also received into the Russian Orthodox Church Outside of Russia as a member of

31   "Met. Petros of Astoria: His Life and Struggle, Part II," Greek Orthodox Christian Television YouTube Channel, accessed June 30th, 2023, https://youtu.be/vLt7cY78eaM?t=2562
32   "ROCOR Resolution September 12/25, 1974, Concerning New Calendarist," Russian Orthodox Church Outside of Russia, accessed June 30th, 2023, https://www.theorthodoxarchive.org/post/rocor-resolution-september-12-25-1974

its synod, albeit a non-voting member. In response to a letter written by Metropolitan Petros, Bishop Hilarion (Kapral) of Manhattan wrote the following reply dated March 12th, 1995:

This is to inform you that at the session of the Synod of Bishops our Church, held on Thursday, February 10/23 of this year [1995], your request for a Vicar Bishop and the candidacy of Archimandrite Paul (Stratigeas) were taken into careful consideration. The members of the Synod have given a positive response to your request for an assistant Bishop, but they wish to take more time to become better acquainted with Archimandrite Paul before making a decision concerning his candidacy. In any case, please be assured that you will be given a Vicar, that the Synod of Bishops values very much your presence within its episcopate, and that it will not abandon you and your Diocese in a time of need.[33]

---

33   Anastasios Hudson, *Metropolitan Petros of Astoria: A Microcosm of the Old Calendar Movement in America* (Reston: Anastasios Hudson, 2014), 66.

Left to Right: Metropolitan Petros of Astoria, Bishop Nektary of Seattle, St. John of San Francisco, Archbishop Averky of Jordanville, Bishop Savvas of Edmonton, Archbishop Leonty of Chile, August 16th, 1963.

Saint Catherine of Attica

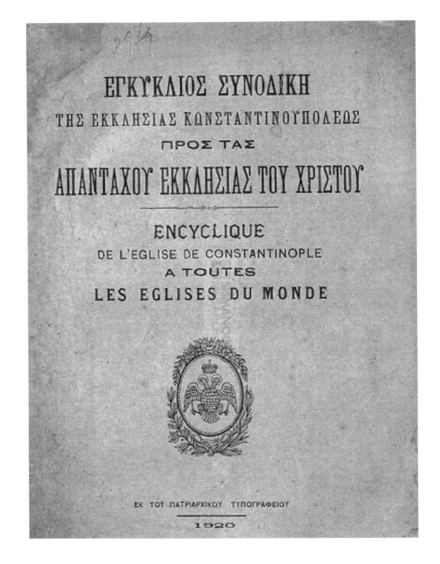

Encyclical of the Ecumenical Patriarchate: "To the Churches of Christ Wheresoever They Might Be" 1920.

Ὁ Τοποτηρητὴς τοῦ Πατριαρχικοῦ Οἰκουμενικοῦ Θρόνου Κωνσταντινουπόλεως † Μητροπολίτης Προύσης Δωρόθεος

† Ὁ Μητροπολίτης Καισαρείας Νικόλαος
† Ὁ Μητροπολίτης Κυζίκου Κωνσταντῖνος
† Ὁ Μητροπολίτης Ἀμασίας Γερμανός
† Ὁ Μητροπολίτης Πισιδείας Γεράσιμος
† Ὁ Μητροπολίτης Ἀγκύρας Γερβάσιος
† Ὁ Μητροπολίτης Αἴνου Ἰωακείμ
† Ὁ Μητροπολίτης Βιζύης Ἄνθιμος
† Ὁ Μητροπολίτης Σηλυβρίας Εὐγένιος
† Ὁ Μητροπολίτης Σαράντα Ἐκκλησιῶν Ἀγαθάγγελος
† Ὁ Μητροπολίτης Τυρολόης καὶ Σερεντίου Χρυσόστομος
† Ὁ Μητροπολίτης Δαρδανελλίων καὶ Λαμψάκου Εἰρηναῖος

*Signatures of the Synod of the Ecumenical Patriarchate on the
Heretical Encyclical of 1920.*

37

Synod of the Russian Orthodox Church Abroad, 1959.

Seated from the Left: Parthenios of the Cyclades (the first to be ordained by Archbishop Leonty), Akakios (Papas) of Talantion (ordained by Seraphim of Chicago and Theophil of Sevres - participated in the consecrations of Archbishop Leonty), Auxentios of Gardikion (the second to be ordained by Archbishop Leonty). Standing from the Left: Akakios of Diavelia (ordained by Parthenius and Auxentius), Chrysostomos (Naslimes) of Magnesia (the third ordained by Archbishop Leonty) and Gerontius of Salamis (ordained by Akakios (Papas) and Auxentius)

38

Left to Right: Bishop Seraphim of Caracas (ROCOR), Bishop Petros of Astoria (GOC), Archbishop Leonty of Chile (ROCOR) at St Markella's after the ordination on November 29th, 1962.

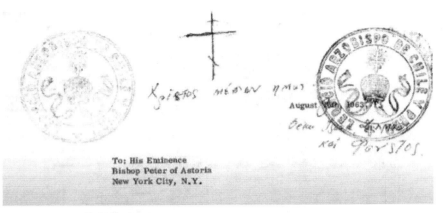

To: His Eminence
Bishop Peter of Astoria
New York City, N.Y.

Your Eminence:

The undersigned are herewith presenting to Your
Eminence the expression of their most sincere gratitude
for your kind reception and hospitality.

May the Lord have Your Eminence in his protection!

Your loving brothers in Christ,

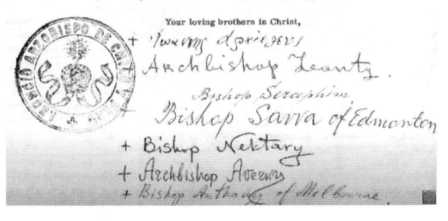

*Photo of the Letter to Bishop Petros Courtesy of
Greek Orthodox Christian Television*

Left to Right: Metropolitan Gerontios of Piraeus and Salamis, Metropolitan Philaret of New York, Archbishop Auxentios of Athens, & Metropolitan Petros of Astoria

Τὸ πρωτότυπον

Архиерейский Синодъ
Русской Православной Церкви
заграницей.

18/31 Декабря 1969 г.

№ ....
75 East 93 St. New York 23. N. Y.
Phone: LEhigh 4-1601.

Его Блаженству,
Блаженнѣйшему Авксентію,
Архіепископу Истинно Православныхъ
Христіанъ въ Греціи.

Ваше Блаженство,

Братское посланіе Вашего Блаженства отъ 25 ноября 1969 г. было нами прочитано въ засѣданіи Архіерейскаго Синода сего числа.

Многія испытанія, какія Православная Церковь переживаетъ съ начала своей исторіи, особенно сильны въ наше лукавое время и потому въ особенности требуютъ единенія между тѣми, кто истинно преданъ вѣрѣ Отцовъ. Съ такими чувствами мы извѣщаемъ увѣдомить Васъ, что Архіерейскій Синодъ Русской Православной Церкви Заграницей признаетъ дѣйствительность архіерейскихъ хиротоній Вашего предшественника, блаженнопочившаго Архіепископа Акакія и послѣдующія хиротоніи Епископовъ Вашей Святой Церкви. Въ соотвѣтствіи съ этимъ и принимая во вниманіе различныя другія обстоятельства, нашъ Архіерейскій Синодъ разсматриваетъ Вашу Іерархію какъ братьевъ во Христѣ, находящихся въ полномъ общеніи съ нами.

Благословеніе Божіе да почіетъ на всемъ клирѣ и вѣрующихъ Вашей Церкви, особливо въ грядущій дни Рождества во плоти Господа и Спаса нашего Іисуса Христа.

Предсѣдатель Архіерейскаго Синода.

+ Митрополитъ Филаретъ

+ Членъ Синода Секретарь + Лавръ, Епископъ Манхаттенскій.

Σημ.: Ἡ σφραγὶς τοῦ ἀνωτέρω ἐγγράφου εἶναι ἀνάγλυφος

Letter from the Russian Synod of Bishops Recognizing the Old Calendarist Ordinations

"We are in full communion with the Greek Old-Calendarist jurisdiction of Archbishop Auxentios in Athens and with the Catacomb Church in Russia; with other jurisdictions our relations are strained, and in some cases broken altogether." - Father Seraphim (Rose), Letter 253, 1978.

Metropolitan Petros of Astoria Serving Hierarchal Liturgy as Proistamenos at Holy Trinity Monastery in Jordanville, New York.

Blessed Metropolitan Philaret of New York, First-Hierarch of the Russian Church Abroad (1903-1985)

*Metropolitan Petros & Bishop Hilarion (Future First-Hierarch of the ROCOR)
February 18th, 1996, at Saint Isidoros Greek Orthodox Church in New York.*

*Left to Right: Bishop Auxentios, Archbishop Chrysostomos, Archbishop Laurus,
Metropolitan Vitaly, Archbishop Anthony, and Archbishop Hilarion.*

46

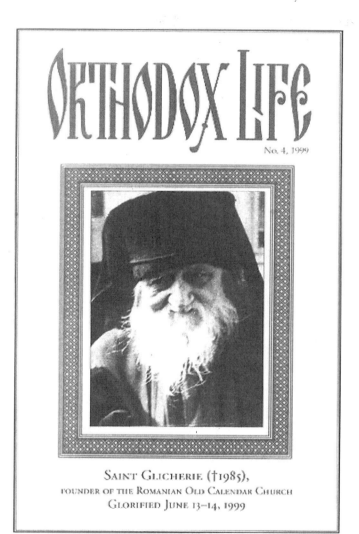

*Orthodox Life, No. 4. 1999. From Holy Trinity Monastery, Jordanville,
New York.*

Left to Right : Mitred Protopriest Alexander Lebedeff (ROCOR) His Grace Bishop Photius of Triaditsa (B-GOC), 2006.

*Blessed Metropolitan Philaret of New York First-Hierarch of the
Russian Church Abroad (1903-1985)*

Chapter IV

The Russian Orthodox Church Abroad & Her True Sister Churches

Over the course of time the Hierarchs of the Russian Synod had become weary of the constant turbulence that the Old Calendar situation created and while communion with the Old Calendarists was still there, it was on shaky ground. In 1993 the Synod of Bishops under the leadership of Metropolitan Vitaly published a resolution (No. 3/50/86) that resolved to "consider the previous decision of the Council of Bishops of the Russian Orthodox Church Outside of Russia, dated Sept. 6/19, 1975, concerning the refraining from concelebration with the hierarchy and the clergy of the Old-Calendarist jurisdictions of Greece, as remaining in effect until unity is achieved among these various Greek jurisdictions."[34]

This was done because of the constant in-fighting that again began to occur within these Old Calendar jurisdictions in Greece. However, this ceasing of concelebrations was short lived. "On 28 June/11 July 1994, the Council of Bishops of the Russian Orthodox Church Outside of Russia addressed the question of the possibility of entering into communion in prayer and the Eucharist with the group of Old Calendarist Greeks headed by Metropolitan Cyprian."[35] A committee which consisted of Archbishop Laurus and Bishops Daniel and Mitrophan was established to examine this. "After deliberation and analysis of all aspects [...] the

34   "Resolution of the Council of Bishops (No. 3/50/86) May 31st, 1993," Russian Orthodox Church Outside of Russia, accessed June 30th, 2023, https://www.theorthodoxarchive. org/post/rocor-synodal-resolution-on-traditional-old-caledndarist-churches-of-greece-may-1993-no-30-50-86

35   "Extract from the Minutes of the Council of Bishops of the Russian Orthodox Church Outside of Russia, 28 June/11 July 1994," Russian Orthodox Church Outside of Russia, accessed June 30th, https://www.theorthodoxarchive.org/post/extract-from-the-minutes-of-the-council-of-bishops-of-rocor-june-1994-concerning-the-goc

Council of Bishops holds that at the present time, when apostasy is spreading and many official representatives of Orthodoxy, such as the Patriarchate of Constantinople and other patriarchates, are succumbing to and embracing the position of the modernists and ecumenists, it is very important for the true Orthodox to unite, stand together and oppose the betrayers of the Orthodoxy of the Holy Fathers. In connection with this, the Council of Bishops has decided:

1. To establish communion in prayer and the Eucharist with the Greek Old Calendarist Synod of Metropolitan Cyprian, as well as with His Grace, Bishop Photios of Triaditsa, who heads the Bulgarian Old Calendar diocese.

2. All parties refrain from interfering in each other's internal ecclesiastical affairs. If any questions arise which require deliberation, it is essential to take counsel together.

RESOLVED: 1) To communicate the above-cited decision to Metropolitan Cyprian and Bishop Photios.

2. To inform our clergy and flock of the Council's decision through publication in church periodicals.[36]

And so, through God's providence, the relationship with the Old Calendarist Greek, Romanian and Bulgarian Orthodox Churches was again regularized and in full Eucharistic communion with each other. In 1996 the fraternal bond with the Greek Old Calendar Church here in the United States grew even stronger when Archbishop Chrysostomos of Etna and Bishop Auxentios of Photiki were invited to co-consecrate Father Gabriel (Chemodakov), now Archbishop Gabriel of Montreal, to the Holy Episcopate. As recorded in the journal published by the Center for Traditionalist Orthodox Studies, Orthodox Tradition, "with the

---

36   "Extract from the Minutes of the Council of Bishops of the Russian Orthodox Church Outside of Russia, 28 June/11 July 1994," Russian Orthodox Church Outside of Russia, accessed June 30th, https://www.theorthodoxarchive.org/post/extract-from-the-minutes-of-the-council-of-bishops-of-rocor-june-1994-concerning-the-goc

blessing of Metropolitan Cyprian, Archbishop Chrysostomos of Etna, and his assistant, Bishop Auxentios of Photiki, travelled to the Holy Trinity Monastery in Jordanville, New York, to participate in the Consecration of Bishop Gabriel of Brisbane, who will serve as an assistant to Archbishop Hilarion of Sydney, recently appointed by the Russian Orthodox Church Abroad to administer its parishes and monastic communities in Australia and New Zealand.

Archbishop Chrysostomos and Bishop Auxentios were invited to take part in the Consecration by Metropolitan Vitaly and Archbishops Laurus and Hilarion. His Eminence, Archbishop Anthony of San Francisco and Western America also took part in the moving and beautiful ceremony."[37]

---

37   Archimandrite Akakios, "Consecration of New ROCA Bishop for Australia," Orthodox Tradition, no. 2 & 3 (1996): 73-74. https://www.theorthodoxarchive.org/post/consecration-of-bishop-gabriel-chemodakov-by-roca-assisted-by-met-chrysostomos-bishop-auxentios

Chapter V

Mutual Recognition of a Saint of the Old Calendar Church

On Saturday and Sunday of June 13th and 14th in 1999, "The Romanian Old Calendar Church Glorified its founder Metropolitan Glicherie (†1985) who struggled against the calendar innovation and the political ecumenism of the Romanian Patriarchate. The Glorification of this contemporary Martyr and Confessor of the Faith, whose amazing spiritual presence (not to mention the many miracles that surrounded his person even before his death) earned him the reputation of being the St. Seraphim of the Romanian Old Calendarists, took place at the Monastery of the Transfiguration in Slatioara, Moldavia, where faithful and clergy from around the world — from Greece, France, Italy, Sweden, the United States, Georgia, Jerusalem, Bulgaria, Australia, Austria, and Africa — gathered for the moving ceremonies."[38]

This issue of Orthodox Life, an official publication of the Brotherhood of Saint Job of Pochaev at Holy Trinity Monastery in Jordanville, New York, was published in 1999 in honor of the newly canonized saint of the Romanian Old Calendar Orthodox Church, Saint Glicherie. He is similar to those saints of the Russian Orthodox Church Abroad, such as blessed Metropolitan Philaret of New York, who were against the modernism that was encroaching on the Orthodox Church everywhere and who struggled against the heresy of ecumenism that was officially anathematized in 1983 by the Holy Synod of the Russian Church Abroad. This glorified saint of the Old Calendarist Romanian Orthodox Church is to this day still held to be a God-ordained saint

---

38   Archimandrite Luke (Murianka), "The Glorification of St. Glicherie of Romania," *Orthodox Life* 49, no. 4 (July-August 1999), 2. https://app.box.com/s/81gdt3nt88e268rf8z5409e77ii cdnxb

by the Russian Orthodox Church Abroad, the Church of the Genuine Orthodox Christians of Greece, and the Old Calendar Orthodox Church of Bulgaria.

Chapter VI

The End of the Road: The Tragic Sundering of Eucharistic Communion

In the late 1990s and early 2000s the Synod of the Russian Orthodox Church Outside of Russia had been in dialogue with the Moscow Patriarchate concerning reunification of the two Russian jurisdictions after eighty years of separation. This dialogue and eventual but sudden reunification with the Moscow Patriarchate was not well received by all within the Russian Church Abroad. The concerns that the Moscow Patriarchate was still a member of the World Council of Churches, was still actively participating in the heretical ecumenical movement (which the ROCOR under the Synod of blessed Metropolitan Philaret of New York had officially anathematized) and the question of Sergianism (which was never officially repented of) weighed on the minds of many.

This became a problem among the Old Calendar Sister Churches which were in full eucharistic and prayerful communion with the Russian Synod. This reunification of the Russian Synod with a jurisdiction which represented everything they were resisting was a pill that could not be swallowed. As 2007 drew near, many letters were exchanged between all of the Synods involved. "Mitred Protopriest Alexander Lebedeff was sent to Romania and Bulgaria for official visits with the Heads of the Romanian and Bulgarian Old-Calendar Churches [...] Fr Alexander read the letter addressed to His Eminence by the Synod of Bishops of the Russian Orthodox Church Outside of Russia and signed by His Eminence Metropolitan Laurus, and heard his response, which expressed the opinion of the Old-Calendar Romanian Church. [...] Fr Alexander was also able to attend divine services at the monastery at the episcopal residence, and also at the large Old Calendar Cathedral of Sofia" and then departed back to the United States.[39]

In the final letter from Metropolitan Cyprian of the Church of the Genuine Orthodox Christians of Greece to the Holy Synod of the Russian Orthodox Church Abroad he writes in the last paragraph:

With inexpressible sorrow, but also in the hope that the Grace of the Mother of God, through the intercessions of St. John Maximovitch [of Shanghai and San Francisco], the most holy Metropolitan Philaret, and all the Russian New Martyrs, will awaken anew your Patristic zeal, so that your Holy Synod might prove once again to be an estimable force, a fortress and a fortified city, and a shield and breastplate of Orthodoxy in our truly apocalyptic times, we remain, as the least among Orthodox Hierarchs,

† Metropolitan Cyprian of Oropos and Fili,

President of the Holy Synod in Resistance"[40]

In two final letters to the primates of the Old Calendarist Orthodox Churches of Romania and Bulgaria after the unification with the Moscow Patriarchate, Metropolitan Laurus addresses them as fellow Orthodox Christian Hierarchs saying, "We asked Your Grace to approach the process of reconciliation with the Church in Russia with the understanding and recognition that this is an internal matter of the Russian Church. Our earnest convictions lead us to the fact that the process of the rebirth of the Church in our much-suffering Homeland after the fall of the godless regime is so firmly rooted and broad, by Divine mercy, that we cannot remain on the outside but must join with it. We have no intention of abandoning our confession of true Orthodoxy before the world, and

---

39   "A Representative of the Synod of Bishops Meets with the Heads of the Romanian and Bulgarian Old-Calendar Churches," Russian Orthodox Church Outside of Russia, accessed June 30th, 2023, https://www.synod.com/synod/eng2006/4enrombulgrep.html

40   "Protocol No. 412. To the Holy Synod of the Russian Orthodox Church Abroad Per His Eminence, Metropolitan Laurus, New York, U.S.A.," Old Calendar Orthodox Church of Greece: Holy Synod in Resistance, accessed June 30th, 2023, https://www.imoph.org/Administration_en/E1a4009Syn412Eng.pdf

will continue to condemn both destructive ecumenism and modernism" and with this the end of the road came and another tragic separation of Orthodox Christians from each other was created.[41,42]

41   "The Synod of Bishops Sends a Letter to Bishop Photii of the Bulgarian Old Calendar Church," Russian Orthodox Church Outside of Russia, accessed June 30th, 2023, https://www.russianorthodoxchurch.ws/synod/eng2007/7enposlphotii.html
42   "The Synod of Bishops Sends a Letter to Metropolitan Vlasie of the Romanian Old-Calendar Church," Russian Orthodox Church Outside of Russia, accessed June 30th, 2023, https://www.russianorthodoxchurch.ws/synod/eng2007/7enposlvlasie.html

Chapter VII

Epilogue

As we can see, the historical relationship between the Russian Orthodox Church Outside of Russia and the Old Calendar Churches of Greece, Bulgaria and Romania were anything but simple. The ecclesiastical history between these Churches extends over a period of eighty years and is clouded with obscurity, biases from multiple sides, resentment, anger, animosity, sinful passions, different perspectives on major theological and ecclesiological issues, language barriers, buried documents that have either been purposefully hidden or accidentally lost, and history that has been forgotten by people within the Church who have become more a-historical over the course of a century. However, what has been made clear by the Russian Orthodox Church Abroad is that these Orthodox Christians in the various Old Calendar jurisdictions, who stood at the holy altar and shared in the most sacred mystery with towering figures of Holy Orthodoxy such as Saint John (Maximovitch), Blessed Metropolitan Philaret (Voznesensky), and Archbishop Averky of Jordanville, to name a few, are in fact just that — Orthodox Christians.

The historical events over this course of eighty-years have most certainly shaped how the Old Calendar Christians are perceived within the Orthodox Christian world even to the present day. This perception can be seen from two different worldviews originating from two different parts of the world. For those in Greece, there has been much animosity and hostility by Old Calendarists, understandably, toward those in the New Calendar State Church because of the persecution the Old Calendarists underwent by the Greek government and under the influence of the State Church of Greece, which also through a constant propaganda campaign demonized them as extremist zealots. Whereas in the United States, from the perspective of the Russian Orthodox Church Abroad, the relationship between the two Churches was much more regular, civil and as a matter of fact Orthodox in nature. Like all behavior, biases, and preconceived notions, these things are learned from somewhere and often are adopted without giving any critical analysis as to why we have adopted a specific worldview. We have to ask ourselves, is what we know about the Old Calendarist Orthodox true or have we adopted a subconscious animosity that has no basis in historical reality and truth?

We also have to examine what it means to be an Orthodox Christian. Does being an Orthodox Christian encompass in our behavior the hurling of accusations of being schismatics or heretics to those who maintain the faith of Holy Ecumenical Councils and the dogmas of the Holy Orthodox Church while the majority of other local Churches have adopted the heresy of ecumenism and participate openly without shame or consequence? This, of course, cannot be justified. And for those within the Russian Orthodox Church Abroad, would we dare stand in judgment of our God-bearing and saintly forefathers, many of whom lay incorrupt in their repose, concerning their judgment of the Old Calendarist Orthodox Christians? Lord have mercy on us if we were to be so bold.

Instead, let us follow the example of the Church Fathers and the Holy Synod of the Russian Orthodox Church Outside of Russia and strive for true unity and peace in Christ our Lord.

"For the Stability of the Holy Churches of God, and for the Unity of All, Let Us Pray to the Lord"

Appendix I

The Glorification of Saint Glicherie of Romania

On Saturday and Sunday, June 13 and 14 (o.s.), the Romanian Old Calendar Church Glorified its founder Metropolitan Glicherie (†1985) who struggled against the calendar innovation and the political ecumenism of the Romanian Patriarchate. The Glorification of this contemporary Martyr and Confessor of the Faith, whose amazing spiritual presence (not to mention the many miracles that surrounded his person even before his death) earned him the reputation of being the St. Seraphim of the Romanian Old Calendarists, took place at the Monastery of the Transfiguration in Slatioara, Moldavia, where faithful and clergy from around the world — from Greece, France, Italy, Sweden, the United States, Georgia, Jerusalem, Bulgaria, Australia, Austria, and Africa — gathered for the moving ceremonies. The Glorification Liturgy on Sunday, attended by twenty thousand believers, was celebrated by fifteen Bishops, ninety-two priests, twenty-six deacons, and scores of servers. Presiding at the Holy Synod of the True (Old Calendar) Orthodox Church of Romania and a spiritual son of the newly-glorified saint; His Eminence Metropolitan Cyprian, President of the Synod in Resistance True (Old Calendar) Orthodox Church of Greece, who was a close spiritual friend of St. Glicherie; and His Eminence, Bishop Photii, Chief Hierarch of the True (Old Calendar) Orthodox Church of Bulgaria.

Metropolitan Cyprian and his entire Synod of Bishops, with the exception of Bishop Chrysostomos of Christianopolis (who was left to attend to the administration of the Church in Greece) and Metropolitan Giovanni (who was prevented by age and infirmity from traveling), attended the services, accompanied by fifty-two laymen from Greece. In addition to the two Bishops from our Exarchate [i.e., the Old Calendarist Greeks] in America, some thirty-five clergy and faithful from the United States were also in attendance. Bishop Photii was accompanied by sixty of his clergy and faithful, as well.

The pilgrims from our Exarchate spent several days before the glorification visiting a number of the one hundred and thirty parishes, thirteen large monastic communities (each with eighty to one hundred and thirty monastics), and many smaller sketes and hermitages belonging to the Old Calendar Romanian Church. In every parish and community, the pilgrims were treated to beautiful meals — virtual banquets — received with overwhelming warmth and hospitality, and were showered with gifts. They left Romania deeply impressed by the piety, dedication, and fidelity of the world's largest Orthodox Church in resistance.

Life of Saint Glicherie of Romania

S aint Glicherie was born on February 9, 1891, in Bucovina, near the ancient castle of Suceava in the village of Mihoveni, to the poor farmers Nicholas and Rachel Tanase. He was baptized in honor of St. George, the patron saint of those who plow and work the land. His father passed away when George was still an infant, and he lost his mother when he was only seven years old. George was brought up by his grandfather, Hilarion Tanase, who had worked for the railroads and was now caring for a boyar's vineyard outside Iasi. His grandfather took the boy to this home in the village of Miroslava; however, George did not find the maternal succor that he needed, since his grandmother, Anna, had long since died. Nonetheless, his grandfather, Hilarion, being a pious Christian, nurtured in him faith in God, which would be his greatest and holy comfort in his future life. Every Sunday and on feastdays, his grandfather took him to pray in a church in the neighboring village of

Comesti, about seven miles from his home.

His grandfather also took him and other children of the village to observe the age-old traditions surrounding the church year. Since George had a quiet disposition and was pious, he was once given the role of a priest in a Christmas play. Another year he played the role of a czar. To some extent, these roles foreshadowed his future — priesthood, monasticism, and in the future, the lofty rank of hierarch. The faithful considered him — and still do — a great and chosen spiritual leader in their land.

At the age of nineteen, George began working at the greenhouse attached to the train station in Ciurea, and later worked at a meat-processing plant in a suburb of Iasi. Six years later, he happened to go to Cetatuia monastery near Iasi to pray. Thirty monks lived at that monastery, and their abbot was Hieromonk Teofil, a spiritual man, kind to strangers. He saw George's devoutness and zeal for the monastic life, and received him as a novice into the brotherhood, providing him with a cell and appropriate clothing. The new novice was so diligent in his duties — being meek, pious, obedient to the Abbot and the other fathers, and respectful — that all considered him worthy to stay. Eight months later, on December 24, 1916 (o.s.), on the eve of the Nativity of our Lord, brother George was tonsured to the small schema with the name Glicherie, which in Greek means "the one who is sweet" or "a man of sweetness." This name truly suited his beautiful spiritual qualities, for his word was sweet and his behavior meek, and all who met him felt this sweetness of character.

Brother George entered the monastery during the First World War. August 15, 1916 Romania entered the war. At the time that Brother George was tonsured, many inhabitants from the South had to flee to Moldavia in the north [the part of Romania where the monastery was located] because of the war. The local population experienced many privations, and it was likewise difficult for the monasteries. Fr. Glicherie fulfilled an obedience in the monastery kitchen, helping to prepare the vegetables, light the fire, or would go into the city to buy necessary supplies. At the same time, he tried not to miss the morning akathists and other services throughout the day.

In 1917, the war moved into Moldavia, bringing with it numerous contagious diseases (e.g., typhus, typhoid fever), which killed many people. Almost all the monastery brotherhood became sick, but Brother Glicherie remained healthy, fulfilling all of his obediences. A temporary hospital was set up at the monastery to care for the sick and wounded soldiers.

One day, Fr. Glicherie saw a soldier stealing vegetables from the monastery garden. In a soft voice, he told the solder that if he needed food or anything else, to ask and he would be given it. But the defiant soldier said that he did not need anyone's approval. The next day, pious Glicherie found the soldier dead under a fence, his hand clutched around a green pepper. Another soldier stole some cucumbers and died in the sick ward with his booty next to him. At that time, Metropolitan Pimen of Moldavia came to the monastery and visited the hospital. He forbade soldiers to steal anything, telling them that the inevitable punishment would befall each one of them.

Fr. Glicherie was ordained hierodeacon on January 11, 1918 (o.s.). He began serving as a hierodeacon not in his own monastery, but in the nearby monasteries of Frumoasa, St. Basil, and St. Nicholas. At the same time, he continued his obedience in the kitchen in his own monastery.

During World War I, Fr. Glicherie had several visions about the future and what the end-result of the war would be. Although he did not particularly understand them at the time, at the end of the war, realizing the similarity between his visions and the events that took place, he related them to Fr. David and those close to him. In January of 1916, a few months before entering the Cetatuia Monastery, he had a vision. It was on a Wednesday, the Eve of Theophany. A large map with the countries of Central Europe appeared to him. Each country had a representative population. Some were kneeling and some (as in Russia), unlike the others, were in rags. The representatives of Romania and Serbia were within their respective boundaries, dressed in beautiful new clothes, and were exceedingly happy. Two days later, on Friday, he had another vision, in which he saw a soldier in a Romanian uniform marching courageously ahead and carrying the Romanian flag towards Bessarabia. When he reached the River Prut, which formed the border between Romania and Russia, a Russian soldier carrying the Russian flag appeared to him and, bowing, surrendered his flag to the Romanian soldier.

In 1920, after the war, Fr. Trifon (Sturza) became the elder of Cetatuia monastery, and gave Fr. Glicherie the obedience of Ecclesiarch, that is, of caring for the church, looking after the services, cleaning, and attending to administration. He fulfilled this obedience and all his other obediences diligently. Seeing this, the elder recommended Fr. Glicherie for ordination to the priesthood. He was ordained on January 29, 1920 (o.s.), on the feast of the holy Apostles, by Metropolitan Pimen of Moldavia.

Soon Fr. Glicherie went to the Great Lavra of the Neamt Monastery [pronounced Ne-á-mets]. The abbot, seeing Fr. Glicherie, rejoiced and kept him at the Lavra for a year, serving in the monastery church and other chapels on feastdays. After a series of transfers to various monasteries and churches, Hieromonk Glicherie was named abbot of the Procrov Skete, which belonged to the Great Lavra at Neamt. The skete was located in the mountains surrounding the Neamt Monastery, and was difficult to reach.

In taking charge of the skete, Fr. Glicherie was given a helper, Hierodeacon David (Bidascu) from the Neamt Monastery. The two bonded spiritually like two brothers, praying and working together, rejoicing and suffering together, and never parting from one another during this earthly sojourn.

When they reached Procrov, they found three old monks and a novice there. Everything was in ruins and monastic order was virtually non-existent. They repaired the cells and restored the ecclesiastical life of the skete with holy and proper prayers. The bells began tolling again, the Typicon of St. Savva was restored, and the monastic life was invigorated.

In 1924, the Romanian Church reformed the Church Calendar and introduced the Gregorian Calendar, already in use by the secular government. It did not, however, alter the celebration of the Feast of Pascha, which was still calculated according to the Julian (Old) Calendar. This marked the beginning of a life of seemingly endless hardship, full of trials and temptations for Hieromonk Glicherie and Hierodeacon David. The change was to occur on October 1 (o.s.), which was to then be considered October 14 (n.s.), the Feast Day of St. Paraskeve, one celebrated with great piety, specially in Moldavia. An order to change the Church Calendar was sent to Procrov as well, with instructions to celebrate the memory of those saints whose Feast Days fell between the first and fourteenth of October, and eliminated, during the following thirteen days, together with the Feast Days of the saints normally celebrated on these days. It was an order, like any other order, administrative or economic. When the order came to the Procrov Skete, which now had twelve monks owing to the spiritual progress of its cenobitic life all with one voice declared that the reform, while fine for astronomy, was not good for the Orthodox Church. The question arose: Why had the other Orthodox Churches not embraced this calendar reform? The change was reckoned a deviation from the Church proper and the Skete continued to serve on the Julian (Church) Calendar dates. It was decided that one of the fathers should search church books for clarification on the matter and consult with ecclesiastical figures conversant in Canon Law and church regulations. Monastic life continued in this way at Procrov from October

1924 through 1925. During this period, the fathers at Procrov had read the epistle of Hieromonk Arsenie (Cotea) of the Holy Mountain of Athos, in which the right-believing faithful of Romania were advised to follow the Church of the East and to flee — to distance themselves — from the New Calendar reform, which he called uncanonical and a capitulation to Roman Catholicism. Soon, Fr. Arsenie went to Romania and visited Procrov, together with Bishop Visarion (Puiu). He subsequently published a book in Romania, Boldurile, in which he condemned the calendar change. After his return to the Holy Mountain, he published other books, The Trumpet of the Hermits and The Interwoven Whip, both dealing with the calendar change. Then, in 1926, a new order, mandating the celebration of Pascha according to the Roman Catholic calculation, was issued.

Great turmoil occurred in the Romanian Church when the Holy Synod decided to change the Paschalion in 1926, and to celebrate Holy Pascha according to the New Style. Determining that this act was uncanonical, since the Canons determine precisely how to calculate the date for the celebration of Pascha each year, in conjunction with the Jewish Passover[43], Hieromonk Glicherie and Hierodeacon David decided to leave Procrov and distance themselves from any other Churches that agreed to celebrate Holy Pascha according to the Gregorian Calendar. The pious Glicherie was summoned to the Neamt Monastery, to which the Procrov Skete belonged, and spoke with Vladyka Nicodim (Munteanu), then Abbot at the Lavra. He advised Fr. Glicherie to adopt the New Calendar, and in exchange he would be made abbot of yet another nearby skete, that of Vovidenia. After discussing this with each other, Fr. Glicherie and Fr. David rejected the offer — earthly glory and ranks are

---

43   The First Ecumenical Council proclaimed anathema (excommunication) on anyone who celebrates the Christian Pascha before or during the first days of the Jewish Passover, which lasts one week. The New Testament Pascha must be celebrated after the Old Testament Passover because it has replaced the Old Testament Passover which was a prefiguration of Christ's Great Sacrifice and Redemption of mankind upon the Cross. Also, Christ resurrected after the first day of Passover of that year, which fell on the Sabbath (i.e., Great and Holy Saturday). Ed.

fleeting. Many others, however, fell to this temptation and departed from the divine teaching of the Lord. The two monks decided that they would not be a stumbling-block on the path of those who decided to celebrate Pascha on the New Calendar. Thus, they left Procrov and went into the mountains, following unchartered trails, until they reached the Coroi Ravine, close to the Sihla Skete, on November 18, 1925 (o.s.). Here, they were far away from the authorities. With great effort, they built a hut, well camouflaged, where they spent the entire winter. In the spring of 1926, they built another hut, bugger and with three rooms — one for a chapel, wherein they could celebrate the church services and recite their prayers.

After some time, three monks joined them from the Sihastria Skete, also in rejection of the calendar reform: Hieromonk Pamvu and two of his brothers, Veniamin and Galaction. They established their huts nearby, and thus a new cenobitic monastic community developed. It is known that almost sixty monks form the Neamt Monastery refused to adopt the New Calendar and, in particular, the alteration of the Paschalion. There was great turmoil in the Lavra.

Life in their hut was very difficult for the two fathers, Glicherie and David, like that of the hermits of old who withdrew from a world full of conniving, confusion, and mishaps. These Romanians, like the ancient hermits, had no desire to harm anyone, but to leave others in peace, according to their convictions, and especially with regard to the celebration of Pascha. In their loneliness, they found solace in work which was undertaken as a monastic obedience. Hieromonk Glicherie would gather mushrooms in the forests, going down to the Neamt Monastery secretly, from time to time, to barter mushrooms for bread, which he would dry. Fr. David would chisel beautifully ornate spoons. They always prayed, no matter how tired they were, and they fulfilled their rule, sometimes at night by candlelight or oil lamps. Though they were often visited by various wild beasts, nothing happened to them.

Fathers Glicherie and David lived in the hut at Coroi Ravine for almost two years, from 1925-1927. After discussing the matter, they decided to go to Mount Athos to worship there, and after earning enough money by working the fields at the Sihla Skete, they travelled to the Holy Mountain. They started their pilgrimage by worshipping at all the Greek, Russian, Serbian, Bulgarian and Romanian monasteries, as well as all of the sketes and smaller kellias, entering into the caves of the Great Athonite hermits as well. An immense joy filled their souls, seeing the great piety of the fathers, with prayers and unceasing services, day and night. In the end, they settled at the Annunciation Skete, which belongs to the great Greek monastery of the Pantokrator, because there was need there for help in their labors. In this way, Fr. David, together with other monks from Romania, worked the lands of the Pantokrator monastery, while Fr. Glicherie served the Divine Liturgy at the Romanian Skete of Prodromul, alternating with the Elder of the skete, Archimandrite Ioasaf. At Prodromul, Elder Ioasaf, a very pious old man, was pleased with the ways of the fathers and tonsured them to the Great Schema.

On the Holy Mountain, the two fathers spent a year in deep silence, praying unceasingly for the forgiveness of sins and the salvation of their souls. No one troubled them and, moreover, all were well disposed to them and embraced them as brothers in Christ. Even the monks of other nationalities, Greeks, Bulgarians, and Serbians, surrounded them with Christian love and helped them. In this blessed garden of the Mother of God, they rejoiced spiritually, and felt protected there against the many temptations of life, as though they were submitting only to God. Having availed themselves of the wonderful Athonite lifestyle, they treasured it, and the example of the Athonite monks was of great benefit to the two fathers, which they tried to emulate for the rest of their lives.

On September 14, 1928, the fathers regretfully left the Holy Mountain of Athos and returned to their homeland, Romania, by ship. Having survived a terrible storm in the Black Sea, to everyone's astonishment, they arrived at the Constanta harbor unscathed. The two fathers then set out towards the Neamt Monastery, to the same hut at Coroi Ravine that they had occupied the previous year. There they were once more united with Hieromonk Pamvu and the other brothers, who rejoiced at the sight of them. Later that autumn, two shepherds happened to discover the huts. After they introduced themselves, the shepherds and monks befriended each other. The shepherds asked Fr. Glicherie to go down to their village.

On January 6, 1929 (o.s.), on the Feast of Theophany, Fathers Glicherie and Daniel, went down to the village and celebrated the Blessing of the Water for some faithful down there. The local priest from Vanatori, Fr. Barliba, found out about this and called the local police, who ransacked the huts at the Coroi Ravine and arrested the fathers. After taking them to police headquarters in the village and mocking them fiercely, the police forced the fathers to go by foot to Tirgu Neamt and, afterwards, to the outpost at Piatra Neamt, where papers were filled out. They were then sent to the city court. This marked the beginning of their troubles.

At the tribunal, the fathers were interrogated regarding their reasons for "hiding" in the forest, and they were asked for the name and whereabouts of the place. They answered rightly, courageously stating that they had done all of this because of the calendar change and, in particular, the change in the date of Holy Pascha, which innovations they considered unlawful. They also said that their place of hermitage was the Coroi Ravine. The judge did not reckon their withdrawal an infraction of the law and thus set them free. The fathers returned to their hut.

During Great Lent that year, Fr. Glicherie descended the mountain with the inhabitants of Vanatori-Neamt to their homes to serve various molebens and to confess them. He selected a particular house and blessed a room therein to be used as a chapel and a place of worship. Many faithful from the village, and even some monks, went there to worship.

Fr. Barliba, the village priest, became angry when he heard about this, seeing that part of his flock was avoiding him, that they were not attending the village church, and that they were going to services celebrated on the Old Calendar, as a result of which, his income was declining. He went to the village police and convinced them that the two fathers were enemies of the state. Thinking that they were defending national interests, the police went up into the mountains and arrested Fr. Glicherie. Returning to the village, they also arrested the two brothers who owned the house containing the chapel. The police put all those arrested in a carriage, along with various liturgical items and books which had been taken from the chapel. Mocking them constantly and blaspheming these holy things, the police took them to Piatra Neamt.

Fr. Glicherie was incarcerated for three months at Piatra Neamt, until the time of this trial, since the priests from Vanatori falsely persuaded the judge that Fr. Glicherie was an uncanonically ordained priest. While there, Fr. Glicherie suffered greatly at the hands of the police. They took him to the basement, where drunken policemen would come at night and beat him, until they were exhausted. During the day, father was forced to wash the floors, while the policemen would climb on his back or beat him so savagely that the walls were covered with his blood. At the trial, several of the monks of the Monastery of Neamt testified that Fr. Glicherie had been canonically ordained and had the Grace of the priesthood. The judge absolved him of any wrongdoing and, in freeing him, returned all of the books and liturgical items that the police had confiscated in such an abusive manner. Being forbidden by the court to return to his hut, Fr. Glicherie remained in Tirgu Neamt in the house of a forest ranger.

This was just the beginning of Fr. Glicherie's many horrible and bloody trials. Wherever he began to serve services for the local population, the police would be tipped off by new-calendar faithful or priests and raids would be made of the house where it was suspected he was serving. Many times, Fr. Glicherie would just narrowly escape arrest, hiding in attics, or fleeing from one house to the next, and from village to village.

In 1929, the celebration of Pascha according to the New Style was to fall on the Second Sunday of [Old Style] Great Lent. Because of this, great spiritual turmoil and upheaval overtook the Romanian Orthodox Christians, to the extent that mass protests were staged by the Romanian populace. Great writers and theologians, such as Nae Ionescu, Nichifor Crainic, Grigore Racoveanu, Nicolae Lupu, and others, declared publicly that the "Holy Synod is schismatic." Therefore, it was decided that the celebration of the Feast of Pascha would be observed according to the old Paschalion and the Julian Calendar. However, there was a counter-reaction to this among those in Romania who wanted to celebrate the Feast according to the New Style. Therefore, the Prime Minister, head of the National Peasant Party and a Uniate (a Greek Catholic, united with the Pope), announced that those priests and bishops who did not celebrate Pascha according to the New Style were free to celebrate it on the Old Style, and the schools, army, and state employees were given a day off. So it was that in many places, the Holy Feast of Pascha was celebrated twice, an error committed even by the clergy. [This highly undesirable situation/This glaring infraction of Canon Law was later rectified when the Romanian Patriarchate, while remaining on the New Calendar for immovable feasts, returned to celebrating Pascha according to the Old Style. ed.]

In the winter of 1930, just before the Nativity, the police, under the influence of a new calendar priest, arrested Fr. Glicherie and Fr. David at Tirgu Neamt, but the two escaped ten days later, on the eve of Theophany. They served for the feast day secretly at the home of the forest ranger. Fr. Pamvu served the Blessing of Water at a fountain near a brook, attended by many of the villagers, while only three men and a few policemen attended services at the village church. In that same year, 1930, the fathers celebrated the Paschal Matins on the traditional date in a meadow, together with a great multitude of faithful, after which they celebrated the Paschal Liturgy in a home of one of the villagers.

In the fall of 1930, Fr. Glicherie went to Jerusalem with a few faithful. Arriving in October, they stayed for six months, until after Pascha. Fr. Glicherie served in many of the Orthodox churches in Jerusalem, but on the second day of Pascha, he was offered to serve with a couple of priests from the Romanian Patriarchate. He refused to serve with anyone who followed the Gregorian Calendar. On Pascha itself, he served at the Russian monastery, along with the Russian Bishop, Anastassy, the last Russian Hierarch of the Archdiocese of Bessarabia.

Back in Romania, Fr. Glicherie lived for a while in Tirgu Neamt. From 1931-1932, the faithful there built a church for services on the old calendar. In 1931, other new churches were built for those faithful to the old calendar. Thus, gradually support and faithfulness to Fr. Glicherie and his refusal to submit to the New Calendar grew among believers in the northern regions of Romania, and became steadily stronger.

On the feast of the Holy Apostles, Fr. Glicherie served at the church in Radaseni. After the feast, all who had participated in the service were taken to the police station. Meanwhile, the village priest called the police to have Fr. Glicherie arrested. The police surrounded the house, and as Fr. Glicherie was running from the rear, they caught up with him just as he was jumping the fence. The fence being old and rotten, it fell under the weight of his pursuers, which incited the policemen to fury. They viciously kicked Fr. Glicherie with their boots and beat him with their rifles. When they lifted him up to drag him under the fence and away, the owner of the house, Vasile Onofrei, came home. He tried to free father, but was threatened by a policeman with a rifle. The other policemen fired warning shots in the air, since several women were also approaching the scene. Vasile Onofrei snatched the weapon out of the policeman's hands, who could not defend himself, since a woman, Ana Grecu, had set upon him with a pitchfork. The rifle shots attracted other villagers and the policeman who had been attacked grabbed a pitchfork and ran towards the others, arresting a monk and an old man in the process. They beat these men up, thinking that one of them was Fr. Glicherie.

Seeing that they had made a mistake, the police returned to the house, where the faithful were hiding Fr. Glicherie and tending to his numerous wounds. A number of policemen tried to force their way into the courtyard, but the gate was locked by a woman who simply clobbered them with a heavy wooden club when they tried to jump the fence. Their captain was also struck, which somewhat tempered their enthusiasm. After the police withdrew, a contingent of peasants marched to the City Hall to protest the abuses committed by the law enforcement officers.

In the winter of 1933, Fr. Glicherie printed the Psalter and other booklets in Suceava. A parish house and various churches were built, and with the help of God, all other churches that were started earlier were finished in that year. All these building projects were supervised by Fr. Glicherie. He was joined by Fr. David and two monks from Mount Athos, and together began serving daily.

Another example of the growing support and following that was mounting around Fr. Glicherie was that in 1934, after the winter holidays, when a rumor circulated to the effect that the police were coming again to arrest Fr. Glicherie and the other priests, the people began to organize themselves. Some guarded the church day and night, while others read the psalter continuously. Everyone had food to eat, if only one meal a day on fast days.

Another time, when Fr. Glicherie and a few priests were on their way to a village near Nemteni to bless a chapel, they were hostilely intercepted by the new calendar village priest and peasants. As Fr. Glicherie's group fled, the aggressors caught one of them and savagely beat him, breaking one of his arms. Hearing of this, Fr. Glicherie's supporters from several villages in the area massed together and went to Nemteni to punish the village priest. Fr. Glicherie stopped them and pacified them, telling them not to counter bad deeds with unchristian ones, but to give evidence to everyone that they were peaceful, God fearing people.

The wound that Fr. Glicherie received when he was beaten and dragged under the fence by the police began to worsen, causing him great pain in the affected leg. This wound never healed and bothered him the rest of his life. Sometimes, father was miraculously spared from pain during the Holy Mysteries, as was the case one year at the feast of St. Paraskeve. Being barely able to carry the icon during the Vigil, he prayed with tears to the saint, and the pains ceased. Another time, he was confined to his bed in Brusturi, his leg hurting him so badly that he could not touch his foot to the floor. A man came to him and asked him to commune an old woman who was dying. He tried to get out of bed, but fell right back, the pain was so great. The man understood and left, but came right back since the woman's condition had taken a turn for the worse. Again, father could not go. Alone, he began thinking about how to resolve his dilemma, as he did not want the woman to die without taking Holy Communion. He tried to walk again and, wondrously, the pain ceased. He then went to the church, gathered the Holy Mysteries, and walked like a healthy man for one and a half miles to the old woman's home. He communed her and returned home. As he stepped across the threshold, the pain started again and he had to lie down on the bed. After a quarter of an hour, the church bells tolled, announcing the death of the old woman.

In the fall of 1935, Fr. Glicherie and Fr. Ghimnazie decided to go to Mount Athos. The goal of their trip was to persuade an Old Calendar Hierarch to accompany them back to Romania. Overcoming many obstacles put in their path by the authorities, they finally reach the Holy Mountain in 1936. There they learned that the authorities had ordered that Old Calendarist monks coming from Romania were to be closely followed through the agency of the Vatopedi Monastery, the only Athonite institution to have accepted the calendar innovation. They did not succeed in their goal, but decided to stay in hiding there during Great Lent. After Pascha, Fr. Glicherie went to Athens, where a Synod of Old Calendarist Bishops was soon to be convened. They had hoped that the hierarchs would consecrate one of the fathers from the Holy Mountain to the Episcopacy. The hierarchs, however, could do nothing without the approval of Metropolitan Chrysostomos of Florina, who had gone to Jerusalem to meet with the Patriarch. Fr. Glicherie and his entourage waited for two months in Athens for a decision. Meanwhile, the Archbishop of Athens, who had adopted the New Calendar, petitioned the British authorities to detain the President of the Old Calendarist Synod of Bishops in Palestine (which was a British Protectorate) and thus prevent him from returning to Athens.

Therefore, Fr. Glicherie and Fr. Ghimnazie decided to return to Romania once more, through Serbia. Due to passport problems, Fr. Ghimnazie had to return to Athens, while Fr. Glicherie met the Russian Archbishop Anastassy (whom he had met before in Jerusalem) in the Russian exile church of the Holy Apostles. When Fr. Ghimnazie finally arrived, the Archbishop advised them to go to Budapest, where the Russian Bishop Seraphim, who had ordained priests in Chisinau, was staying. According to the Archbishop, Bishop Seraphim could go to Romania and ordain Old Calendarist priests there, if need be. Reaching Budapest, the fathers found the Russian church closed and learned that Bishop Seraphim had gone to Vienna. Arriving in Vienna, they met the Bishop, who was without a church and who was fearful of going to Romania. He finally refused to go, so Fr. Glicherie and Fr. Ghimnazie, after much travel, exhaustion, and expense, went back to Bucharest.

The Romanian faithful were overjoyed to see Fr. Glicherie in their midst again, and immediately asked him to bless the sites of several new churches. When he left the last town in this series of blessings, he encountered a bus with papered up windows and full of policemen.

They tried to detain Fr. Glicherie, but they could not, since more than a thousand people gathered and surrounded him. Fr. Glicherie finally reached his own house in Brusturi. The police found this out and, after midnight, went to apprehend him. They went to the church on foot. Jumping the fence, they found three men in the courtyard who, while guarding the place, had fallen asleep. The policemen kicked them, beat them with their rifles, and tried to enter the church. Fr. Glicherie had been walking towards the belfry with his brother, Antonie. They quickly began tolling the bells. The village was awakened and, finding the police bus, the villagers smashed the windows. There was a tremendous uproar, with shouts and cries everywhere. Shots were fired. Seeing that the entire village was up in arms, the policemen, sensing danger, withdrew. Such was the greeting prepared for Fr. Glicherie upon his return to his homeland.

On September 1, 1936 (o.s.), Fr. Glicherie, along with his followers, took part in the consecration of the church in Buhalnita (in the Neamt District). They left for the service in five hundred wagons, with almost four thousand of their countrymen. Being met with great joy and with flowers by the villagers, Fr. Glicherie celebrated the blessing of the church, the beautiful services lasting many hours. After the celebration, a delegation of faithful from Bodesti came to invite the pious father to bless their church as well. On the way to Bodesti, the multitude (four thousand strong) were met by a truck full of policemen intending to stop them, but when they saw the number of people, they turned and left in fear. The procession was stopped at the entrance to Piatra Neamt, on a bridge. A Christian man from another village tried to pass this barrier on bicycle, and was shot in the arm by the police. Infuriated by this, the crowd pushed the policemen aside and forced their way into the city. The police fired more shots, and used tear gas. The people huddled in their wagons and went on their way. Exiting the city, they were met by firemen, who began spraying them with their pressure hoses. The situation became desperate when the army appeared and began firing their machine guns.

People were running in every direction. Fr. Glicherie and Fr. David ran into an orchard, but the former had to hide under a bush on account of the wound on his leg. Finally they got to the backyard of a Jew who hid them in his shed. The police found Fr. David and beat him so badly, that he suffered the rest of his life from these wounds. The Jew eventually turned in Fr. Glicherie. The police came, dragged him out to the shed, and began hitting him in the head with their rubber clubs. When Fr. Glicherie fell, they then kicked him with their boots. When he was thrown into jail, other policemen came and dragged him into a room in which the floor and walls were covered with blood stains form those previously interrogated there.

He spent the whole night there, after which, in the morning, they took him to the police station. There, they dressed the wounds that literally covered his body and took photographs of him. They clothed him in a military uniform, with a coat and a cap. His face was completely bandaged, except for his eyes, so that he would not be recognized. That night, they put him in a car and escorted by the Chief of police from Piatra Neamt, left for an unknown destination. They stopped in a forest, and Fr. Glicherie was sure he would be shot right there. But the journey continued. Putting him on a train, Fr. Glicherie was eventually delivered to the Ministry of the Interior, where reporters and photographers were waiting. They took pictures of him, but avoided photographing his swollen and bloody hands.

Fr. Glicherie was put in a jail cell. After a few hours, the wife of General Paranianu, the police commander, went to see him. Hearing from Fr. Glicherie the horrible things that had happened, she was moved to pity and began to weep. Later, she sent her servant to Fr. Glicherie with food and some wine. After several transfers, Fr. Glicherie was finally incarcerated in the Iezeru Skete and put in a dark room. After a week, Fr. David and many other jailed people joined him. Fr. Glicherie remained there for six months. He was then transferred elsewhere for a month and then returned again to the Iezeru Skete. At this point, he was informed that he had been sentenced to prison for one year. Being transferred every few days to a new place, father ended up in the jail at Iasi, where he remained for eight months. Finally, he was taken to Iezeru, and then to Piatra Neamt, where he served out a sentence of two more years.

After this, Fr. Glicherie was accused not only of being an "Old Calendarist," but also of being a Communist or a Legionary (a member of the fascist Iron Guard). The reason for this is that the New Calendar priest in Raucesti, trying to convince the authorities to arrest the pious Fr. Glicherie — who was enlightening the minds and hearts of the villagers and thus making it very uncomfortable for those who were preaching falsehood — denounced him for spreading "Old Calendarist propaganda" and inciting the village to embrace Communism and the Legionary movement. His goal was to charge him with a crime subject to capital punishment and thus to be rid of him once and for all — to see the truth wholly disappear. One day in 1939, when Fr. Glicherie was alone in Raucesti, he was arrested by the police major from Piatra Neamt and the chief of police from Tirgu Neamt on these false charges. He was eventually transported to Miercurea Ciuc, a detention camp for Legionaries.

There were eighty Legionaries in this camp. One night in November, nine months after Fr. Glicherie arrived, an order was issued that all of the detainees were to be executed in two groups of forty each, the first group at 4:00 a.m., and the other at 6:00 a.m. Fr. Glicherie was assigned to be shot in the second group. Around four o'clock, he heard some machine gun rounds followed by the cries of dying people. He was already preparing for the bullets. All of the forty remaining were taken to a room to pray. It was exactly six o'clock. Two other priests were with them in the room, each with a cigarette in his mouth and both members of the Iron Guard. They too were going to pray as their lives came to an end. As Fr. Glicherie was on his knees, praying to the Mother of God for the forgiveness of his sins and in gratitude for being able to end his earthly life in the Orthodox Faith of Almighty God, he looked up with tears in his eyes and heard a beautiful voice saying that his life and the lives of all the others who were praying with him would be spared, and that they would be set free. And indeed, a miracle occurred; just before dawn, the government had decided that all of the Legionaries would be spared.

Two months later, a Legionary government came to power. Therefore, anticipating harsh measures, Fr. Glicherie and Fr. David left for the Neamt District, settling near the Procrov Skete of the Great Lavra of Neamt. In a hut they themselves made, they lived there from May till the next February. Learning that the police were still looking for them, they abandoned the hut for higher ground, staying among the rocks where no one could find them.

The police found and destroyed their hut, so in the middle of winter they had to build a new hut in another place, where they stayed until some forest rangers found them in February of 1941. Since the rangers were crude, they feared that they might turn them in. The two fathers left, carrying with them as much as they could, putting the rest in a large container and burying it. Fortunately, they were discovered by a man from the village of Slatioara, in the Suceava District (where the Monastery of the Transfiguration is now located). After establishing contact with the pious villagers of Slatioara, the fathers moved to the neighboring village of Buda to live there in hiding for six months. Some of the villagers of Slatioara built the fathers a hut in the forest next to spring, where they stayed until the end of World War II. The villagers provided them with all their necessities.

After the war, Fr. Glicherie returned among his people and began to build churches again, including rebuilding all those destroyed between 1935 and 1936. At this time, Fr. Glicherie began organizing the building of the monastery in Slatioara, which was to be a refuge for all of those monks and priests who had survived the harsh persecutions. This was facilitated by the fact that the new government made the Church a legal entity, and in this way it was possible to obtain the necessary papers to begin construction.

The year 1947 marked the beginning of the construction of the Slatioara Monastery and the first contacts with Bishop Galaction (Cordun) through a delegation which went to Bucharest. At that time Bishop Galaction was a hierarch of the official Romanian Orthodox Church. They requested that he become the spiritual leader of the Traditional Orthodox Church of the East (in those days, the official name of the Old Calendar Orthodox Church of Romania). By mutual agreement, they decided to postpone his arrival until 1955, when the monastery was to be completed and they could offer him adequate accommodations and facilities for his work.

In 1950, as the Communist Party became stronger, the persecution of the Old Calendarists was revived. These new efforts were principally directed against the Slatioara Monastery, which was considered to be the bastion and center of resistance for the Old Calendarists, whom their enemies had wished to see destroyed from the outset.

During the night from February 1-2, a number of trucks with militia came to the monastery, surrounded it, and arrested everyone. They were all imprisoned at the Danube-Black Sea Channel. Father Teofan died there, while others died in yet other locations. The stamps and official seals of the Church were confiscated from the headquarters in Tirgu Neamt. They received a prison sentence of two years at hard labor, after the completion of which, all of the clergy were freed and returned to the monastery.

When they returned, the Blessed Glicherie initiated the necessary steps to have Bishop Galaction (Cordun) brought to Slatioara, where he had promised to come when the monastery and cells were built. To this end, he sent a delegation to Bucharest, comprised of Fr. Dionisie (Hugeanu), Evloghie Ota, and Silvestru Onofrei. Bishop Galaction received them very cordially and preparations were made for his arrival. On May 21, 1995 (o.s.), in the morning hours, at the tolling of church bells, the one who would become the first Metropolitan of the Old Calendar Orthodox Church of Romania, Bishop Galaction (Cordun), arrived at Slatioara Monastery. He was greeted with the Holy Gospel by Hieroschemamonk Glicherie, Hierodeacon David, the Abbot of the monastery, and a crowd of worshippers and believers. At the end of the Holy Liturgy, the Blessed Hieroschemamonk Glicherie was made an archimandrite, amid praise from Metropolitan Galaction for his struggle to defend what was right, as well as the True Faith. It should be noted that His Eminence's decision to return to the Old Calendar of his own volition, at the request of the faithful was made public by an act notarized in Bucharest, on April 5, 1955 (o.s.), by the State Notary. He assumed the title of "First Hierarch and Metropolitan of the Traditional Orthodox Church of the East." This document was sent to the Romanian Patriarchate, to Patriarch Alexei of Moscow, and to Patriarch Kyrill of Bulgaria, who had been colleagues of his at the Theological Academy in Saint Petersburg. Following this announcement, persecution from the "official" Orthodox Church of Romania began anew.

Within a few days of Metropolitan Galaction's transfer to the Slatioara Monastery, Archpriest Tiu from the Patriarchate, representing the Minister of Cults, arrived at the monastery in a black car with a chauffeur. He was purportedly sent to accompany Metropolitan Galaction and Archimandrite Glicherie to Bucharest, where they were supposedly to receive notification of the legalization of their Church body. Seeing that no one believed him, he fell down on his knees, crying and kissing the Bishop's hand, imploring him and assuring him that he was telling the truth. This convinced no one. Nonetheless, the Metropolitan decided to go to Bucharest. Despite great opposition from the entire community of monks and faithful, who saw that this was a plot to deliver them up to the authorities, Metropolitan Galaction, Archimandrite Glicherie, and Hierodeacon Agafangel left for Bucharest with Archpriest Tiu. After a very long and arduous trip by car, they were delivered up to the Security Bureau in Ploiesti.

After being interrogated, Metropolitan Galaction was sent to Cernica, under house arrest, until the end of the spring of 1956. After this, he was arrested again and sentenced to six months. Fr. Glicherie was sent to Baragan, in the village of Rachitoasa, with other detainees. There he spent his time in an earthen hut.

Contacts with Metropolitan Galaction at Cernica were not impossible, and numerous times the Metropolitan would secretly go to Bucharest to ordain priests. In this way, in the fall of 1956, he consecrated Bishops Evloghie (Ota) and Meftodie (Marinache). It was also decided at this time, that Fr. Glicherie was taken to Slatioara Monastery, where he was never again arrested, despite repeated threats. The Most Reverend Glicherie never left the monastery from that time on.

Vladyka Glicherie maintained a very organized and vigorous schedule, which was followed assiduously. In the evening, he was always at Matins. In the morning, he was the first at the Akathist to the Mother of God, the Hours, and the Divine Liturgy. Often he was present at the daily Memorial Service. Because he was the first in church, it was he who many times lighted the candles and oil lamps. In the summer, after Liturgy, he would work in the vegetable garden, this being a passion since his youth. At two o'clock in the afternoon, he would put aside his hoe and go to his cell, where he observed his personal prayer rule of prayer, in keeping with monastic custom, until the Ninth Hour [i.e., three o'clock. ed.]. Afterward, he would go to the church for Vespers, and then to the refectory, something which he never missed. After the meal, he would rest a little. Later, if he still had something to do in the garden, he would finish it, after which he would attend Compline. When this ended, he would go to this cell for private time, until the appointed hour for Matins.

After Metropolitan Galaction's death, Vladyka Glicherie became the Chief Hierarch of the Old Calendar Orthodox Church of Romania, being raised to the rank of Archbishop and Metropolitan. During this period, Metropolitan Glicherie ably watched over the administration of the Church. There were problems and tribulations that could not be avoided that arose from the arrests of monks and priests. This led to an acute lack of clergy, which obliged Metropolitan Glicherie to send priests from the monastery to substitute in various parishes. This ended between 1963 and 1964, when all of the priests were set free.

A fire broke out in the Slatioara Monastery in March of 1984, in which several buildings and other material goods and food were lost. This and other problems in the life of the Church affected Metropolitan Glicherie's health, not only physical, but especially spiritual, and he began to deteriorate significantly. The wound on his leg became deeper, creating unbearable pain. Still, in spite of the diminution of his physical strength, he put forth an enormous effort to take part in the Patronal Feast of the Slatioara Monastery in 1984 (the Feast of the Transfiguration), participating in the celebrations and anointing and blessing all of the people [it is not unusual for twenty thousand faithful to be in attendance at this celebration, ed.].

During Great Lent of 1985, due to loss of appetite, Metropolitan Glicherie lost a great deal of weight, forcing him to spend more and more time in his cell, immobilized in bed. During this time, since he loved the church services so much, he was deemed worthy to see angels serving at the Divine Liturgy and to see St. George, for whom he had such devotion, having borne his name since Baptism and having read his Akathist every day. Three days before his death, he called together the community, as well as various believers from the village, and blessed them, forgiving them all, like a true father.

On Friday, June 15/28, 1985, shortly before the noonday meal, the monastery administrator, Fr. Vlasie (the present Archbishop and Metropolitan), seeing that Metropolitan Glicherie was very weak, asked him if he desired Holy Communion. His Eminence answered positively. After he had partaken of the Holy Mysteries, he began to breathe heavily. Immediately, the two Bishops, Silvestru and Demonsten, were summoned. They remained at this bedside until 5:40 in the afternoon, when the Blessed Metropolitan Glicherie gave up his soul into the hands of God. Such was the end of the life of this great Confessor and Martyr, who suffered not at the hands of pagans, but at the hands of those who called themselves Orthodox Christians — even clergymen.

Metropolitan Glicherie left behind him a blessing: he left the Church united; and from above, he is watching its good progress. We [the Synod of the Old Calendar Romanian Church] are cognizant of the fact that it is by his holy prayers that the Church is now in full blossom. His martyrdom was not in vain. God rewarded him graciously and blessed his hard work with sixty new churches and monasteries. From what were previously only forty-five priests, there are now one hundred and fifty — all of this within a mere thirteen years of his repose. The total number of parishes has grown from forty to one hundred and ten. During these years, His Eminence has appeared to various people, asking them to tell the church Hierarchy to exhume his remains (he was entombed in the Slatioara Monastery).

After a thorough investigation of all of the reports received, and after consultations by the Holy Synod with bishops from other countries — and especially with Metropolitan Cyprian of Oropos and Fili (Greece), who knew Metropolitan Glicherie during his life — we acknowledged Metropolitan Glicherie to be a Saint and thus preparations for exhumation began. First, with prayer and care, a reliquary was carved by the monks at Slatioara. When all was ready, three days before the memorial of his repose, the tomb was opened. His fragrant bones were exhumed, washed in wine, according to tradition, dried, and anointed with Holy Myrrh, in preparation for the great day of his glorification, which [took place] on June 15/28, 1999.

May God also grant, by his prayers, to all of his followers the same love and fervor that the Blessed Glicherie showed for the Orthodox Church, that together we might inherit heavenly things, in the everlasting Kingdom of God, to Whom is due all prayer love, and glory. Amen.

Condensed with permission of his Grace,

the Right Reverend Auxentius from:

"The Life of the Holy Hierarch

and Confessor Glicherie of Romania,"

by Metropolitan Vlasie, published in English by

the Center for Traditionalist Orthodox Studies,

Etna, California, 1999.

Liturgical Hymns to Saint Glicherie

Troparion, Tone IV:

Confessor of the True Faith,/ Good Shepherd of the Church of
Christ,/ Enlightener of the People of God,/ Blessed Hierarch
Glicherie,/ thou who hast worthily received the crown of Everlasting
Life,/ pray to Christ our God,/ that He might save our souls.

Kontakion, Tone VIII:

O most excellent hierarch of the true Faith,/ defender of the Church
of Christ,/ protect all Orthodox faithful who ever sing to thee:/ rejoice,
O hierarch of Christ, Glicherie,/ most wondrous confessor of the
Lord.

91

Chronology

1920 — The Encyclical "To the Churches of Christ, Whosoever They Might Be" is published by Constantinople, calling for the creation of a common calendar.

1924 — The "Revised Julian" or New Calendar is forced on the State Church of Greece by Constantinople, in cooperation with the Greek Church and state government. Pious laypeople, supported by so-called "zealot" monks from Mount Athos, resist the change and continue to observe the old Patristic Calendar.

1925 — A miraculous appearance of the Holy Cross in the sky occurred over the Church of Saint John the Theologian in Athens on the eve of the Exaltation of the Cross in 1925.

1926 — In April, the State Church condemns the "Old Calendarists" as schismatic and devoid of grace.

- In May, the Greek religious community of Genuine Orthodox Christians is registered to further the cause of restoring the Church calendar.

- Zealot Elder Theodosius of Karoulia enters into dialogue with Metropolitan Anthony (Khrapovitsky). Metropolitan Anthony is sympathetic but discourages severing communion.

1927 — Following a violent police raid on an Old Calendar Church in Athens, St. Catherine Routis is martyred in defense of the Patristic Calendar.

1934 — The Community of the Genuine Orthodox Christians asks Metropolitan Anthony (Khrapovitsky) to receive their parishes under the jurisdiction of the ROCOR. No answer was received.

1935 — Three Church of Greece metropolitans accept the

invitation to lead the over eight-hundred Old Calendar parishes and monasteries. The senior bishop being the retired Metropolitan of Florina, Chrysostom (Kavourides). Anticipating arrest, they consecrate four new bishops, one of whom was the Athonite zealot Archimandrite Matthew (Karpathakis) as Bishop of Bresthena.

1937 — A division occurs over the ecclesial status of the New Calendar Church and the status of their sacraments, with the majority eventually being led by Metropolitan Chrysostomos of Florina whose followers became known as Florinites and a smaller more radical group led by Bishop Matthew whose followers became known as the Matthewites.

1948 — Being alone with few followers other than monastics, Bishop Matthew consecrates four new bishops singlehandedly, thus cementing the Florinite and Matthewite division.

1950 — Bishop Matthew passes away, but his synod lives on with non-canonical bishops.

1954 — Archimandrite Petros (Astyfides), a priest of Metropolitan Chrysostom of Florina, runs into Archbishop Averky of Jordanville and Archbishop Leonty of Chile at Grand Central Station in New York. A lifelong friendship begins.

1955 — Metropolitan Chrysostom of Florina, the last surviving canonical bishop of the Genuine Orthodox Church of Greece, reposes in the Lord.

1959 — The Russian Church Abroad under Metropolitan Anastasius (Gribanovsky) discusses a petition to consecrate bishops for the Florinites but declines for pragmatic reasons.

1960 — Without Synodal approval, Archbishop Seraphim of Chicago, and Bishop Theofil of Sevres consecrate GOC Archimandrite Akakios (Papas) as Bishop of Talantion.

1961 — Archbishop Leonty of Chile travels to Greece and consecrates bishops with Bishop Akakios.

1962 — On Nov. 26th, a Russian Church Abroad Synodal meeting is held to discuss the unapproved consecrations. Bishops are divided.

- On Nov. 29th, Archbishop Leonty of Chile and Bishop Seraphim of Caracas consecrate Fr. Petros (Astyfides) in New York as Bishop of Astoria, again without permission.

- On Nov. 30th, another Synod meeting is held, with the Synod again divided. Officially, the consecrations are not recognized, while many prominent bishops privately support them.

1964 — Metropolitan Anastasius (Gribanovsky) retires, and Bishop Philaret of Brisbane is elected First Hierarch of the Russian Church Abroad.

1969 — All consecrations of the Greek bishops are officially recognized by the Russian Church Abroad. The Church of Genuine Orthodox Christians of Greece under the leadership of Florinite Archbishop Auxentios of Athens is recognized as a Sister Church.

- The Matthewite Metropolitan Kallistos of Corinth initiates a dialogue with Hieromonk Panteleimon (Metropoulos) of Holy Transfiguration Monastery in Brookline, Massachusetts.

1971 — After two years of dialogue and hopes of fostering a union between the two factions of Old Calendarists, Matthewite Metropolitans Kallistos of Corinth and Epiphanios of Kition have their consecrations regularized by ROCOR bishops at the monastery in Brookline. They are then instructed to regularise other Matthewite clergy, which many refused to undergo.

1974 — The Florinite Synod issues an encyclical affirming the same ecclesiological understanding as the Matthewite Synod which states that the New Calendarists are truly schismatic and without sacramental grace.

- The Russian Church Abroad reaffirms previous statements condemning the New Calendar, but leaving questions of grace to a future Ecumenical Council.

- Bishop Petros of Astoria honoring the ecclesiological understanding of the Russian Church Abroad and under the advisement of Metropolitan Philaret of New York refuses to sign the GOC Encyclical of 1974 and is dismissed by the GOC Synod.

1975 — In May, the Matthewite Synod breaks communion with the Russian Orthodox Church Outside of Russia.

- In September, ROCOR decrees to refrain from all concelebrations with Greek Old Calendar clergy from all factions until unity can be achieved in Greece.

1979 — Following disorderly and divisive events in the 1970s, Metropolitan Kallistos of Corinth (now with the Florinites) and another Florinite bishop consecrates eight archimandrites with hopes of replacing other dysfunctional bishops. One of the individuals consecrated was Archimandrite Cyprian (Koutsoumbas) of Sts. Cyprian and Justin Monastery in Fili, Attica.

1984 — Following a series of recriminations and reorganizations, Metropolitan Cyprian of Oropos and Fili establishes his own Synod on the basis of the original ecclesiology of Metropolitan Chrysostomos of Florina, known as the Synod in Resistance.

1985 — Bishop Petros of Astoria is invited back to the Synod of the Genuine Orthodox Church of Greece.

1987 — Bishop Petros is elevated to ecclesiastical rank of Metropolitan (Archbishop).

1993 — The Russian Church Abroad under Metropolitan Vitaly (Ustinov) reaffirms the 1975 decision to refrain from concelebrating with any Old Calendar synod until unity is achieved among themselves.

1994 — Metropolitan Petros is received into the ROCOR Synod as a non-voting member with the title of Archbishop of Astoria.

1994 — A petition is discussed to enter into communion with the Synod in Resistance under Metropolitan Cyprian, and a committee is appointed. Once the committee's work is complete, a decision is made to enter into communion with the Synod of Metropolitan Cyprian, largely on the basis of similar ecclesiological understandings.

1995 — ROCOR acknowledges the desire of Archbishop Petros for a vicar bishop, but wants to become more familiar with the candidate, Archimandrite Pavlos (Stratigeas).

1996 — Bishop Gabriel of Brisbane (now Archbishop of Montreal) is co-consecrated by two bishops of the Holy Synod in Resistance at Holy Trinity Monastery in Jordanville, New York.

1997 — Bishop Petros returns to the GOC Synod following assurances that his chosen successor, Father Pavlos (Stratigeas) would be consecrated. Later in the same year Metropolitan Petros of Astoria reposes in the Lord.

1999 — The Russian Synod recognizes the glorification of Saint Glicherie by the Old Calendar Orthodox Church of Romania.

2006 — Following the years of union talks with the Patriarchate of Moscow, ROCOR Archpriest Alexander Lebedeff travels to Romania and Bulgaria to prepare its then Sister Churches for ROCOR union with Moscow.

2007 — The Russian Orthodox Church Outside of Russia signs a unification document with the Moscow Patriarchate and becomes an autonomous Church within the Moscow Patriarchate.

The former Old Calendar Sister Churches then cease communion with the Russian Church Abroad. No declaration from the Russian Synod has ever been pronounced calling any of its former Sister Churches schismatic, outside of the Orthodox Church, or any of their mysteries invalid.

Glossary

Ecclesiology: The theological doctrine relating to the boundaries of the Orthodox Church.

Florinites: Members of the Synod who fell under the leadership of Metropolitan Chrysostomos of Florina and later maintained his ecclesiology that it was outside the local Church's authority to determine if there is or is not grace in those jurisdictions of the New Calendar Churches and that a future Ecumenical Council will have to judge this particular issue.

GOC: A general acronym which stands for Genuine Orthodox Church. It is a generalized abbreviation that refers to the idea rather than to an individual synodal body.

GOC-K: This ecclesiastical acronym refers to the Genuine Orthodox Christians of Greece under the leadership of Archbishop Kallinikos of Athens and All Greece.

Locum Tenens: One filling an office for a time or temporarily taking the place of another — used especially of a doctor or clergyman.

Matthewites: Members of the Synod who fell under the leadership of Bishop Matthew of Bresthena and today's members of various Matthewite synods who embraced his ecclesiology that all New Calendarist Churches are without grace in their mysteries.

New Calendarists: Those members of jurisdictions who adopted the Gregorian or Revised Julian Calendar Innovation that was promulgated by the Heresiarch Meletios Metaxakis, the Patriarch of Constantinople in 1924.

Old Believers: Russian Orthodox Christians who maintained the liturgical and ritual practices of the Russian Orthodox Church as they existed before the liturgical reforms of Patriarch Nikon of Moscow between 1652 and 1666. The Old Believers broke communion with the canonical Church over these issues. They were later unjustly condemned by the dubious Synod of 1666-1667. In 1971 the Moscow Patriarchate revoked the anathemas which had been issued against them. The Russian Orthodox Church Outside of Russia in 1974 also resolved the Old Believer issue under the leadership of Metropolitan Philaret of New York.

Old Calendarists: Orthodox Christians who belong to jurisdictions that have walled off from those local Orthodox Churches which adopted the New Calendar innovation and participate in the heresy of Ecumenism in the World Council of Churches.

Omophorion: A distinctive liturgical vestment worn only by an Orthodox Christian bishop which is a symbol of his spiritual and ecclesiastical authority. Often Orthodox Christians will refer to themselves as 'under the Omophorion' of a particular bishop, meaning under his ecclesiastical authority and spiritual responsibility.

ROCA: An acronym for the Russian Orthodox Church Abroad. ROCA is generally an older name for the same organization of the Russian Orthodox Church Outside of Russia.

ROCOR: An acronym for the Russian Orthodox Church Outside of Russia.

Sergianism: An ecclesiological heresy that the Moscow Patriarchate adopted in 1927 which pledged obedience to the civil authority and embraced a complete oneness of mind with the Soviet atheistic regime that was simultaneously imprisoning and executing thousands of Russian Orthodox Christians within the USSR. This heresy was established by Metropolitan Sergius on July 20th, 1927.

Sobor: Russian for an ecclesiastical synod, council, or assembly of the Orthodox Church.

TOC: An acronym for the True Orthodox Church, often used interchangeably to refer to Old Calendarist jurisdictions in general but does not generally refer to a specific synodal body.

WCC: An acronym for the World Council of Churches which is a heretical interreligious organization that promotes the heresy of Ecumenism and the idea of one world religion. On its website, the World Council of Churches gives a list of all autocephalous and autonomous Orthodox Churches that are members. The autocephalous and autonomous Orthodox Churches that are not members of this organization as of this writing are:

- Patriarchate of Bulgaria
- Patriarchate of Georgia
- Macedonian Orthodox Church – Archdiocese of Ohrid
- Russian Orthodox Church Outside of Russia
- Ukrainian Orthodox Church (UOC)

Bibliography

"A Contentious Discussion on the Consecration of Greek Old
Calendar Bishops by Archbishop Leonty during the 1962 meeting
of the ROCOR Council of Bishops. The Minutes of Protocol #24,
November 13/26, 1962." Russian Orthodox Church Outside of
Russia. Accessed June 29th, 2023. http://sinod.ruschurchabroad.
org/Arh%20Sobor%201962%20Prot.htm

"A Contentious Discussion on the Consecration of Greek Old
Calendar Bishops by Archbishop Leonty during the 1962 meeting
of the ROCOR Council of Bishops. Minutes of Protocol #28,
November 17/30, 1962." Russian Orthodox Church Outside of
Russia. Accessed June 29th, 2023. http://sinod.ruschurchabroad.
org/Arh%20Sobor%201962%20Prot.htm

Akakios, Archimandrite. "Consecration of New ROCA Bishop for
Australia." In *Orthodox Tradition*, no. 2 & 3 (1996): 73-74. https://
www.theorthodoxarchive.org/post/consecration-of-bishop-gabri-
el-chemodakov-by-roca-assisted-by-met-chrysostomos-bishop-aux-
entios

"A Representative of the Synod of Bishops Meets with the Heads of
the Romanian and Bulgarian Old-Calendar Churches." Russian
Orthodox Church Outside of Russia. Accessed June 30th, 2023.
https://www.synod.com/synod/eng2006/4enrombulgrep.html

Central Intelligence Agency (CIA). "Religion." In American Society
of Civil Engineers & R.I. Society of Professional Engineers
Inc. Accessed August 7th, 2023. https://www.cia.gov/reading-
room/docs/NEW%20ENGLAND%20THE%20CRADLE%20
OF%5B15877520%5D.pdf

This Unclassified CIA Document states something of similar opinion
that was being spoken about inside of the American intelligence
agency during the period. "The Soviets soon found out that they could
not risk keeping the Churches closed and therefore set up a puppet
Church with a puppet Patriarch. This, naturally, did not satisfy the
Russian Orthodox Church and religion went underground. I know
of the existence of thousands of so-called catacomb congregations
in secret places of Russia. In these underground churches the masses
hold religious services, worshipping God and teaching secretly
Theology, and educating missionaries for [Orthodox] Christianity."

"Extract from the Minutes of the Council of Bishops of the Russian
Orthodox Church Outside of Russia, 28 June/11 July 1994."
Russian Orthodox Church Outside of Russia. Accessed June 30th.
https://www.theorthodoxarchive.org/post/extract-from-the-
minutes-of-the-council-of-bishops-of-rocor-june-1994-concerning-
the-goc

Holy Synod of the Russian Orthodox Church Outside of Russia. "To
The Most Blessed Auxentius, Archbishop of the True Orthodox
Christians in Greece." The Orthodox Archive. Accessed June 29th,
2023. https://www.theorthodoxarchive.org/post/50th-anniversary-
of-the-goc-episcopal-consecrations-by-the-russian-church-abroad

Holy Trinity Monastery. "The Enthronement of Metropolitan Philaret." *Orthodox Life* 87, no. 3 (May-June 1964), 6.

Kiriacou, Metropolitan Demetrius. "Questions About the GOC to Metropolitan Demetrius - The Light of ROCOR." Orthodox Tradition - YouTube Channel. Accessed June 16th, 2023. https://www.youtube.com/watch?v=JaQeq4VVtzM

"Letter from Archpriest Gregory Grabbe to Mr. V.M. Shallcross, November 7th, 1973." Synod of the Russian Orthodox Church Outside of Russia. Accessed June 30th, 2023. https://www.theorthodoxarchive.org/post/bishop-gregory-grabbe-to-mr-shallcross-concerning-metropolitan-kallistos-and-ephiphanios-1973

"Letter No. 98. To Hieroschemamonk Theodosius of Mount Athos." Азбука веры. Accessed June 28th, 202. https://azbyka.ru/otechnik/Antonij_Hrapovickij/pisma/#0_100

"Letter No. 99. To Hieroschemamonk Theodosius." Азбука веры. Accessed June 28th, 2023. https://azbyka.ru/otechnik/Antonij_Hrapovickij/pisma/#0_101

Mannis, Nikolaos. *The Ecclesiology of the Metropolitan Chrysostomos: Presentation of the Ecclesiological Positions of the Former Florentine Confessor, Chrysostomos (Kavouridou) (†1955) in the Form of Questioning.* Athens: Genuine Orthodox Christians of Greece, 2012.

Mark, Gloria. "Speaking of Psychology: Why our attention spans are shrinking, with Gloria Mark, PhD." American Psychological Association. Accessed June 16th, 2023. https://www.apa.org/news/podcasts/speaking-of-psychology/attention-spans

"Met. Petros of Astoria: His Life and Struggle, Part II." Greek
    Orthodox Christian Television YouTube Channel. Accessed June
    30th, 2023. https://youtu.be/vLt7cY78eaM?t=2562

"Met. Petros of Astoria: His Life and Struggle, Part II." Greek
    Orthodox Christians Television YouTube Channel. Accessed Au-
    gust 28th, 2023. https://youtu.be/vLt7cY78eaM?si=Nnm5IiNpTK-
    WZ28bp&t=1999

Metropolitan Philaret of New York. "About the New Martyrs and the
    Gracelessness of the Soviet False Church," circa 1964-1985,
    Russian Orthodox Church Outside of Russia, Audio Recording,
    23:29. From the Private Library of Subdeacon Nektarios Harrison,
    M.A.

There were many people within ROCOR and among the Hierarchs
who believe that the Moscow Patriarchate was a USSR Soviet creation
and not the actual legitimate Church. Metropolitan Philaret of New
York and later Metropolitan Vitaly (Ustinov) were among those with
this opinion. Metropolitan Philaret of New York is quoted saying:
"But here's what I wanted to draw your attention to, something
that many people don't think about at all. Father Archimandrite
Konstantin, probably many of you know him, the late editor of the
magazine Orthodox Rus, is a deep, Christian mind, he considered the
most terrible of all the communists' "achievements" that communism
created its own false church, the Soviet one, which they suggested
to the unfortunate people instead of the real Church, that went into
the catacombs, disappeared from the surface. Do not think that I
am exaggerating, or that Father Konstantin exaggerated. Once there
was an All-Russian Church Council, in 1918. At this Council, the
entire All-Russian Church, headed by its Primate Patriarch Tikhon,
anathematized (excommunicated from the Church) both the enemies
of God themselves and all those who would cooperate with them."

Murianka, Archimandrite Luke. "The Glorification of St. Glicherie of Romania." *Orthodox Life* 49, no. 4 (July-August 1999), 2.

"New Zion in Babylon: The Orthodox Church in the Twenti eth Century (Part III)." Dr. Vladimir Moss, PhD. Accessed June 27th, 2023. https://www.academia.edu/10287412/NEW_ZION_IN_BABYLON_PART_3_1925_1941_

"Protocol No. 412. To the Holy Synod of the Russian Orthodox Church Abroad, Per His Eminence, Metropolitan Laurus, New York, U.S.A." Old Calendar Orthodox Church of Greece: Holy Synod in Resistance. Accessed June 30th, 2023. https://www.imoph.org/Administration_en/E1a4009Syn412Eng.pdf

"Resolution of the Council of Bishops (No. 3/50/86) May 31st, 1993." Russian Orthodox Church Outside of Russia. Accessed June 30th, 2023. https://www.theorthodoxarchive.org/post/rocor-synodal-resolution-on-traditional-old-caledndarist-churches-of-greece-may-1993-no-30-50-86

ROCOR Resolution September 12/25, 1974, Concerning New Calendarist." Russian Orthodox Church Outside of Russia. Accessed June 30th, 2023. https://www.theorthodoxarchive.org/post/rocor-resolution-september-12-25-1974

Rodzianko, Michael and Vsevolod, Rassaphor-Monk. *The Truth About the Russian Church Abroad.* Jordanville: Printshop of St. Job of Pochaev - Holy Trinity Monastery, 2002.

The Canons of the Holy and Altogether August Apostles. "Canon I." In *Nicene & Post-Nicene Fathers, Volume 14*, edited by Philip Schaff & Henry Wace. Peabody: Hendrickson Publications, 1999.

"The Development of Russian Orthodox Church Outside of
Russia's Attitude Toward Other Local Orthodox Churches and
Non-Orthodox Christians." ROCOR Studies: Historical Studies
of the Russian Church Abroad. Accessed June 28th, 2023. https://
www.rocorstudies.org/2008/11/18/the-development-of-russian-
orthodox-church-outside-of-russias-attitude-toward-other-local-
orthodox-churches-and-non-orthodox-christians/

The Holy Orthodox Church in North America. *The Struggle Against
Ecumenism: The History of the True Orthodox Church of Greece from
1924-1994*. Boston: Holy Transfiguration Monastery, 1998.

"The ROCOR Debate at the 1959 Council of Bishops on
Consecrating Hierarchs for the Greek Old Calendarists - Protocol
#15." Russian Orthodox Church Outside of Russia. Accessed June
29th, 2023. http://sinod.ruschurchabroad.org/Arh%20Sobor%20
1959%20Prot10-16.htm

"The Synod of Bishops Sends a Letter to Bishop Photii of the
Bulgarian Old Calendar Church." Russian Orthodox Church
Outside of Russia. Accessed June 30th, 2023. https://www.
russianorthodoxchurch.ws/synod/eng2007/7enposlphotii.html

"The Synod of Bishops Sends a Letter to Metropolitan Vlasie of the
Romanian Old-Calendar Church." Russian Orthodox Church
Outside of Russia. Accessed June 30th, 2023. https://www.
russianorthodoxchurch.ws/synod/eng2007/7enposlvlasie.html

Index

A

Akakios (Papas), Archbishop, 22-23, 30, 38, 93, 94

Alexander of Berlin, Archbishop, 20

Anastasius (Gribanovsky), Metropolitan, 16, 19-20, 22-23, 25, 29, 93-94

Anthony (Khrapovitsky), Metropolitan, 12-16, 29, 92

Anthony of Geneva, Bishop, 20-21

Anthony of Los Angeles, Bishop, 20

Anthony of Melbourne, Bishop, 26-27

Archbishop Akakios (Papas). See Akakios (Papas), Archbishop.

Archbishop Alexander of Berlin. See Alexander of Berlin, Archbishop.

Archbishop Athanasius of Buenos Aires. See Athanasius of Buenos Aires, Archbishop.

Archbishop Averky (Taushev) of Syracuse. See Averky (Taushev) of Syracuse, Archbishop.

Archbishop Chrysostomos of Etna. See Chrysostomos of Etna, Archbishop.

Archbishop Laurus (Škurla). See Laurus (Škurla), Archbishop.

Archbishop Leonty of Chile. See Leonty, Archbishop of Chile.

Archbishop Seraphim of Chicago. See Seraphim of Chicago, Archbishop.

Archpriest George Grabbe. See George Grabbe, Archpriest.

Astyfides, Archimandrite Petros of Astoria. See Petros (Astyfides) of Astoria, Archimandrite.

Athanasius of Buenos Aires, Archbishop, 23

Auxentios of Athens, Archbishop, 41, 94

Auxentios of Photiki, Bishop, 52-53

Averky (Taushev) of Syracuse, Archbishop, 2, 6, 19-21, 24, 26-27, 35, 61, 93, 119

B

Basil Stamatoulis, 16

Bishop Anthony of Geneva. See Anthony of Geneva, Bishop.

Bishop Anthony of Los Angeles. See Anthony of Los Angeles, Bishop.

Bishop Anthony of Melbourne. See Anthony of Melbourne, Bishop.

Bishop Auxentios of Photiki. See Auxentios of Photiki, Bishop.

Bishop Hilarion (Kapral) of Manhattan. See Hilarion (Kapral) of Manhattan, Bishop.

Bishop Nektary of Seattle. See Nektary of Seattle, Bishop.

Bishop Nikon (Rklitsky). See Nikon (Rklitsky), Bishop.

Bishop Savva of Edmonton. See Savva of Edmonton, Bishop.

Bishop Seraphim of Caracas. See Seraphim of Caracas, Bishop.

Bishop Theophil of Detroit. See Theophil of Detroit, Bishop.

Bishops, Council of, 24-26, 32-33, 51-52

C

Canon 13, 13

Catacomb, 23, 43, 103, 105

Catherine Routis, Saint. See Routis, Catherine.

Chrysostom of Florina, Metropolitan, 11, 80, 93, 95, 115

Chrysostom of Zakynthos, Metropolitan, 11

Chrysostomos of Etna, Archbishop, 52-53

Churches,
    Greek, 21, 23, 25, 92
    Sister, 29, 51, 57, 94, 96, 97

Commemoration
      Ceasing, 12, 15

Communion, 31
    Accepted into, as bishops, 31
    Break (ceasing), 13, 15, 31-32, 92, 95, 97, 99
    Come into, 2, 9, 30, 51, 52, 96

G

George Grabbe, Archpriest, 31

Genuine Orthodox
    Church of America, 32
    Church of Greece, 11, 12, 16, 93, 95

Germanus of Demetrias, Metropolitan, 11-12

George Paraschos, 16

Glicherie of Romania, Saint, 55, 65-91, 96

H

Hieroschemamonk Theodosius of Mount Athos. See Theodosius of Mount Athos, Hieroschemamonk.

Heresy, 1, 3, 7, 10, 19, 33, 55, 62

Hilarion (Kapral) of Manhattan, Bishop, 34, 46, 53

Holy Trinity Monastery, 19-20, 44, 47, 53, 55, 96

J

John (Maximovitch) of San Francisco, Saint, 6, 20-21, 24, 26, 35, 58, 61,

L

Laurus (Škurla), Archbishop, 46, 51, 53, 57-58

Leonty, Archbishop of Chile, 19-20, 22-27, 35, 38-39, 93-94,

M

Markella, Saint, Church of, 19, 23, 26, 39

Matthewites, 21, 31, 93

Meletios Metaxakis. See Metaxakis, Meletios.

Metaxakis, Meletios, 10, 15, 98

Metropolitan Anthony (Khrapovitsky). See Anthony (Khrapovitsky), Metropolitan.

Metropolitan Chrysostom of Florina. See Chrysostom of Florina,

Metropolitan.

P

R

S

Metropolitan Chryostomos of Florina

115

Saint Ieronymos of Aegina

Saint John the New Almsgiver & Wonder-Worker

Saint Glicherie of Romania

Archbishop Nikon, Metropolitan Philaret, Archbishop Averky
Holy Ascension Cathedral in the Bronx, 1965.

Glory to God for All Things!

.

Made in the USA
Middletown, DE
06 November 2023

41890138R00073